Gift-wrapped In Swaddling Cloths

**Sermons On The
Second Readings
For Sundays In
Advent, Christmas,
And Epiphany**

Robert S. Crilley

CSS Publishing Company, Inc., Lima, Ohio

GIFT-WRAPPED IN SWADDLING CLOTHS

Copyright © 2003 by
CSS Publishing Company, Inc.
Lima, Ohio

All rights reserved. No part of this publication may be reproduced in any manner whatsoever without the prior permission of the publisher, except in the case of brief quotations embodied in critical articles and reviews. Inquiries should be addressed to: Permissions, CSS Publishing Company, Inc., P.O. Box 4503, Lima, Ohio 45802-4503.

Scripture quotations unless marked otherwise are from the *New Revised Standard Version of the Bible*, copyright 1989 by the Division of Christian Education of the National Council of the Churches of Christ in the USA. Used by permission.

For more information about CSS Publishing Company resources, visit our website at www.csspub.com or e-mail us at custserv@csspub.com or call (800) 241-4056.

ISBN 0-7880-1984-8   PRINTED IN U.S.A.

*To my wife Judith Ann,
who allows me to experience the same love
that these sermons attempt to express*

Table Of Contents

Advent 1   7
    Just You Wait!
    1 Thessalonians 3:9-13

Advent 2   13
    Burden Or Blessing?
    Philippians 1:3-11

Advent 3   19
    God's Peace Is On Patrol
    Philippians 4:4-7

Advent 4   25
    The Ultimate Sacrifice
    Hebrews 10:5-10

Christmas Eve/Christmas Day   31
    Gift-wrapped In Swaddling Cloths
    Titus 2:11-14

Christmas 1   37
    Forgiveness
    Colossians 3:12-17

Christmas 2   43
    God's Benefactors
    Ephesians 1:3-14

Epiphany 1   49
(Baptism Of The Lord)
    Crossing Borders And Breaking Down Boundaries
    Acts 8:14-17

Epiphany 2   **55**
Ordinary Time 2
    The Multitasking Church
    1 Corinthians 12:1-11

Epiphany 3   **63**
Ordinary Time 3
    Not Just Any Body, Christ's Body
    1 Corinthians 12:12-31a

Epiphany 4   **69**
Ordinary Time 4
    Losing That Loving Feeling
    1 Corinthians 13:1-13

Epiphany 5   **77**
Ordinary Time 5
    Sharing What We Have Been Shown
    1 Corinthians 15:1-11

Epiphany 6   **83**
Ordinary Time 6
    The Son Also Rises
    1 Corinthians 15:12-20

Epiphany 7   **89**
Ordinary Time 7
    Revised And Amended By The Author Of Life
    1 Corinthians 15:35-38, 42-50

Epiphany 8   **95**
Ordinary Time 8
    A Labor Not In Vain
    1 Corinthians 15:51-58

Transfiguration Of The Lord   **101**
(Last Sunday After Epiphany)
    The Glory That Shines Within
    2 Corinthians 3:12—4:2

Lectionary Preaching After Pentecost   **107**

U.S. / Canadian Lectionary Comparison   **109**

Advent 1
1 Thessalonians 3:9-13

Just You Wait!

Some of you may be excited to learn that this morning's scripture lesson contains a benediction. "Now may our God and Father himself and our Lord Jesus direct our way to you. And may the Lord make you increase and abound in love for one another and for all, just as we abound in love for you. And may he so strengthen your hearts in holiness that you may be blameless before our God and Father at the coming of our Lord Jesus with his saints" (vv. 11-13). That is a benediction. And the reason it may excite some of you is because when you start out with a benediction, the sermon can't be very long. (It will only seem so!)

This particular benediction refers to an event commonly known as the "Second Coming." The Bible, incidentally, never uses that phrase; and to be honest, I've always been a little troubled by it, because it seems to suggest that Christ is only returning one more time — at some point in the distant (or not-so-distant) future. Until then, he's sitting idly backstage waiting for the final curtain call. Obviously, though, nothing could be further from the truth. Christ is very much with us even now. Whenever people gather together in his name, our risen Savior is present. But as Christians, we also believe that, at the end of history, he will arrive again triumphantly, and every knee will bend in heaven and on earth, and every tongue will confess that Jesus is Lord, to the glory of God (Philippians 2:10-11).

It's actually a subject that Paul discusses quite a bit in this letter. He tells the Thessalonians that "the Lord himself, with a cry of command, with the archangel's call and with the sound of God's trumpet, will descend from heaven, and the dead in Christ will rise first. Then we who are alive, who are left, will be caught up in the clouds together with them to meet the Lord in the air" (1 Thessalonians 4:16-17a). A little later, Paul borrows an image from one of Jesus' parables and explains that "the day of Lord will come like a thief in the night ... So then let us not fall asleep as others do, but let us keep awake" (1 Thessalonians 5:2, 6).

Traditionally, of course, this idea of "keeping awake and alert" has served as the theme for the First Sunday of Advent. It is a time for us to ponder and prepare, to watch and wait. However, it's not just Christmas that we're waiting for. Unlike the culture that surrounds us, the church has never been in a great hurry to get to Christmas. Indeed, all of the lectionary texts for this morning focus not so much on the past, but toward the future.

In our Gospel Lesson from Luke, for example, Jesus tells the disciples, "There will be signs in the sun, and the moon, and the stars, and on the earth distress among the nations confused by the roaring of the sea and the waves. People will faint from fear and foreboding of what is coming upon the world, for the powers of the heavens will be shaken. Then they will see 'the Son of Man coming in a cloud' with power and great glory" (Luke 21:25-27). In our Old Testament Lesson from Jeremiah, the prophet announces, "The days are surely coming, says the Lord, when I will fulfill the promises I made to the house of Israel and the house of Judah. In those days and at that time I will cause a righteous Branch to spring up from David; and he shall execute justice and righteousness in the land" (Jeremiah 33:14-15). And here in our Epistle Lesson, Paul writes, "May he so strengthen your hearts in holiness that you may be blameless before our God and Father at the coming of our Lord Jesus with his saints" (v. 13).

What these passages are getting at is that, despite all appearances to the contrary, the world is not just stumbling blindly along, or spinning wildly out of control. There is a heavenly purpose that God is working out here on earth. Just as the universe had a definite beginning, it will also have a definite and intentional end. There will come a time when the last pages of history have been written, and everything is revealed beneath a light that casts no shadows, and we will find ourselves standing before a court beyond which there is no further appeal. Simply put, there will eventually arrive a judgment day in which all of our days, and all the judgments upon us, and all of our judgments upon each other, will themselves be judged. The creator of all things will become the completer of all things.

I'm not sure what you happen to think about the end time. But if you are like most folks, you probably don't think about it much. Frankly, the whole notion of the Second Coming tends to confuse a lot of us. I remember in seminary, my New Testament professor J. Christiaan Beker once shared with the class a revealing and amusing correspondence from an official mainline denominational magazine. A reader had submitted a question to the "Question and Answer" column, which was subsequently answered by one of the editors:

> *Q: Why are there so few sermons in our churches on the Second Coming? Is this part of our belief or not?*
>
> *A: Not all Christians think alike on matters of theology, but it would be hard for someone to feel at home in our tradition who did not understand God as the One who has come, who is present (Christ is risen) in our lives today, and who is yet to come in whatever form the future winds up taking. To literalize the Second Coming is to ruin both its beauty and its significance. To ignore it is to avoid what may be the most important part of the Gospel we know about since the past and present, relatively speaking, are brief, while tomorrow borders on forever.*

In a later issue of the magazine, another reader responded to this answer:

> *I compliment the Rev. _____ for his illusive non-answer to what I am sure was a serious question concerning the Second Coming of Jesus Christ. If I understood his answer, he said, in effect, "We don't all agree.*

> *But if you want to be comfortable in the [United Church of Christ and Presbyterian Church], you will need to agree that Jesus is coming again, but not really — for if you actually believe in the Second Coming you will ruin both its beauty and significance. Yet you can't ignore it because it's in the future." Why not a simple answer? Why not admit that those who cannot receive the Bible literally must spiritualize the Second Coming because it is too large a segment of the New Testament to be ignored?*[1]

This reader makes an excellent point. Either we believe that Christ is coming again — literally, physically, historically — or we don't. Of course, part of the problem with dwelling on it is that not many of us are eager to be associated with those placard-carrying prophets-of-doom who are forever announcing that the world is going to end on such-and-such date. We may affirm a literal interpretation of the Second Coming of Jesus Christ, but we're not inclined to pour over the pages of our Bibles with a calculator, trying to pin God down to a specific timetable. After all, it's supposed to be a journey of faith, not a scavenger hunt. Every rumor of war in the Middle East, every leadership change in Russia, every currency crisis in the stock market, does not need to set loose another riptide of Armaggedon anxiety. Jesus himself said, "About that day and hour no one knows, neither the angels of heaven, nor the Son, but only the Father" (Matthew 24:36).

At a deeper level, though, the problem with waiting in eager anticipation for the Second Coming is that the church has already been waiting for some 2,000 years now. If it is to occur like a thief breaking into your house at night, that would seem to imply that we must be ready at all times, because we can never be sure when Christ will break into the world, or even when he will break into our lives. But therein lies the difficulty. It is almost impossible to be on a high state of alert 24/7. You can only stand on tiptoe searching the horizon for so long, before you grow weary of looking toward a future that seems to be taking its sweet time getting here. In other words, even if we concede that no one knows for certain when Christ will come again, we're still left with the question of what to do in the meantime.

I think Paul's benediction may provide a clue. Notice that he is not telling the Thessalonians that, since Christ is on his way, they can close down their food pantry for the homeless and stop collecting special offerings. Waiting for the Second Coming is not like sitting in a concert hall, casually passing the time until the house lights are lowered and the conductor takes the stage. It is more like waiting for an honored guest to arrive at our home. There is much to do; everything must be made ready. Thus, Paul's prayer for the Thessalonians is that their love for each other, and for everybody else, may increase and abound (v. 12). Keep watching for Christ's arrival, sure; but don't stop working, says Paul. Be prepared, not passive.

Far from lifting the church out of the world, the belief that our risen Lord will surely come again ought to send the church back into the world with renewed confidence and conviction. To live in hopeful expectation of the future appearing of Christ does not mean that we give up on the present world, filled as it is with sickness and starvation, pollution and poverty, warfare and waywardness. On the contrary, the reason Christians work so hard to rid the world of such things is because we know that the same One who will finally vanquish the powers of darkness at the end of time is already moving in mighty strength against them even now.

The other day, on the way home from a hospital visit, I heard a rather intriguing statistic on the radio. In the game of chess, after each person has made one move, there are roughly 400 possibilities for the next move. After a player has moved twice, there are over 70,000 possibilities. With three moves, the number increases to more than nine million. That surprised me, because I would have thought it to be just the opposite. That is, the greatest number of possibilities exists before you do anything, and the longer you play the fewer the options you have available. But the fact is, the more moves you make, the greater the options.

Perhaps the future is like that as well. No one can be sure exactly when the Second Coming will occur. But in the meantime, we keep moving. We keep working, and praying, and serving, and loving one another. Because who knows? Maybe the more we do, the greater the possibilities that God is able to do something through us.

Every First Sunday of Advent, we are reminded of the need to stay awake and watch. Ordinarily, we take that to mean, "Don't abandon your lookout post. Keep your eyes fixed upon the horizon. Watch and wait." But there is another way to hear the word "watch" — as in the statement, "You think that was something? Watch this!" Maybe what Paul is trying to tell the Thessalonians is: "Open your eyes. Pay attention. Watch what God is able to do, if you keep working, and praying, and serving, and loving one another. And may he so strengthen your hearts in holiness that you may be blameless before our God and Father at the coming of our Lord Jesus with his saints."

Is Jesus Christ returning again with power and great glory? Absolutely. But if you think a baby in a manger was something, you ain't seen nothing yet. Just you watch ... just you wait!

---

1. This exchange is recorded in J. Christiaan Beker, *Paul's Apocalyptic Gospel* (Philadelphia: Fortress Press, 1982), pp. 12-13.

Advent 2
Philippians 1:3-11

Burden Or Blessing?

There is an ancient Chinese parable that goes like this:

> *There was once a farmer who lived in a tiny, country village. He was regarded as extremely fortunate because, unlike most of the villagers, he owned a horse. One day, though, his horse got loose and ran away. The neighbors all exclaimed how terrible this was, but the farmer responded, "Burden or blessing — who's to say at this point?" A few days later the horse returned, bringing two wild horses with it. His neighbors began to rejoice at this surprising turn of events, but the farmer simply said, "Blessing or burden — who's to say at this point?" The next morning the farmer's son tried to ride one of the wild horses. However, the horse threw him and broke the son's leg. The neighbors offered their sympathy at the farmer's misfortune, but he again replied, "Burden or blessing — who's to say at this point?" The following week conscription officers arrived in the village to enlist young men for the army. They rejected the farmer's son because of his broken leg. When the neighbors told the farmer how lucky he was, he answered, "Blessing or burden — who's to say?"*

What this story suggests is that the meaning of any event is largely a matter of perspective. That is, the arrival of two wild horses is viewed by the villagers as fortunate, until it is seen in the context of the son's broken leg. Likewise, the broken leg seems to be bad in the context of a peaceful village; but when considered from the perspective of conscription and war, it suddenly becomes good. It's almost as if the event itself is neither good nor bad. It all depends on how you look at it.

To use another analogy, suppose you were to see a sign in a store window that read, "We Sell and Repair Watches." Most of us would immediately assume that this is a jeweler's shop. Maybe so, but if we applied a different frame of reference, we might discover that it is actually a shop which makes signs. A subtle shift of perspective, therefore, can often result in a radical change of meaning.

Among psychologists this technique is known as "reframing," and it has proved particularly helpful for people who are struggling with depression because they feel stuck in an intractable situation. It's not a matter of their being lost or confused. It's more that they think they've run out of options and have nowhere to turn. As hopeless as their dilemma may seem, however, by shifting the frame of reference and allowing them a different perspective on the problem, sometimes new possibilities can emerge. What was previously understood as an obstacle suddenly becomes an opportunity.

The reason I mention this is because long before psychologists coined the term "reframing," the Apostle Paul appears to have already been practicing it. In his letter to the Corinthians, for instance, he points out that we presently view life as "in a mirror, dimly, but then we will see face to face" (1 Corinthians 13:12a). In other words, if we are having a difficult time making sense of things, it could be because we're not seeing the whole picture. We lack perspective, and hence, when we come across a detour, we tend to think of it as just that — a detour. But when we've reached our final destination, suggests Paul, we'll be able to look back over the journey, and perhaps consider ourselves extremely fortunate that the path suddenly went one way rather than another. Burden or blessing — who's to say at this point?

Possibly the best scriptural example of this is the Old Testament story of Joseph and his brothers. As you recall, Joseph was Jacob's favorite son. So much so, in fact, that he didn't have to work in the fields with his brothers. Instead, he was free to spend his days and nights dreaming of future glory. That was hard enough for his brothers to stomach. However, when Joseph kept recounting these dreams in sickening detail at the breakfast table each morning, they quickly lost their appetite for him altogether.

Their initial plan was to toss him into a pit and tell the old man that his fair-haired boy had had a fatal tangle with a wild animal — thereby killing most of Jacob's dreams as well. But when some traveling salespeople happened by, they saw a chance to be rid of Joseph and turn a tidy profit besides. He eventually wound up as a slave in Egypt working for an army captain named Potiphar. After a brief stint in jail over an embarrassing misunderstanding with his employer's wife, Pharaoh got word that Joseph had a knack for interpreting dreams, and decided to see if the young Israelite could decipher some troubling ones that he'd been having lately. Joseph passed the exam with the same flying colors that had once adorned his coat, and Pharaoh promptly gave him a cabinet position as head of the Department of Agriculture.

Years later, when a famine struck up north, Joseph's brothers were forced to make the trek down to Egypt themselves. Because they had pretty well put him out of their minds, they didn't realize that it was Joseph at first. But he recognized them, and couldn't resist the opportunity of pretending that they were spies, just to settle the score. The charade didn't last long, however, since Joseph was starving for family as much as they were for food. When he finally revealed who he was, they fell into each other's arms — laughing and crying and swapping stories — almost as if it had all been a bad dream. "Don't be afraid," Joseph reassured them. "You may have intended to do me harm, but God intended it for good" (Genesis 50:20).

In effect, Joseph reframed his entire life. Instead of seeing his brothers' treachery as a burden, he came to understand it as a blessing. And I think Paul is trying to do the same thing in his letter to the Philippians. Those of you who are familiar with this epistle know that he is writing it from a prison cell. We're not sure what precipitated his arrest or even what the accusations were, but inasmuch as imprisonment was for persons awaiting trial rather than a punishment following conviction, Paul's fate is now in the hands of the Roman authorities.

The Philippians, of course, are anxious to hear how he is faring. However, what they need from Paul is more than simply a news report. The fact that their pastor is sitting in jail has the whole congregation talking, and it requires some explanation. No doubt, the unbelieving community was already offering its interpretation, just as it had for the crucifixion of Jesus. "If this man were really the Son of God," the crowds murmured, "God would have rescued him." Likewise, some may have pointed out that if Paul were really following God, these painful and humiliating defeats would not keep occurring.

There have always been those who believe that there is a direct correlation between the kind of person you are and what happens to you. In fact, it is still popular in many Christian circles today to promote faith in God as the key to health, happiness, and prosperity. Very likely then, there were some in Philippi who were starting to wonder whether the church was really that good a deal. After all, what's the point of being Christian, if it doesn't offer you a measure of protection and security?

Make no mistake; Paul needs to interpret his current circumstances. In the first place, it will help silence his critics. But more importantly, almost any suffering or injustice can be endured if we are able to make sense of it. If some higher purpose is being served, most of us can tolerate whatever life throws our way. However, there is no pain quite as stinging as that which has no explanation, and no tragedy so heavy as the one where we are left groping in the darkness searching for what it all means.

Notice, though, how Paul goes about interpreting this for the Philippians. "I want you to know, beloved," he writes, "that what has happened to me has actually helped to spread the gospel, so that it has become known throughout the whole imperial guard and to everyone else that my imprisonment is for Christ" (Philippians 1:12-13). A little later, he confides to them that he hasn't quite made up his mind whether he wants to be released or executed. "I'm not sure which I prefer," he admits. "I am hard pressed between the two: my desire is to depart and be with Christ, for that is far better; but to remain in the flesh is more necessary for you" (Philippians 1:23-24).

What an extraordinary thing to say! You would think that the choice was his to make. But since Paul is neither judge nor jury, his opinion one way or the other is of no consequence whatsoever. If any of us were to get a letter from a friend on trial informing us that they were having a difficult time figuring out whether to be sentenced or set free, we would seriously begin to question our friend's state of mental health. Has Paul suffered too much or simply too long? What is he talking about here? He has absolutely no decision in this matter. On the contrary, he is awaiting someone else's decision.

And yet, in another sense, Paul does have a decision to make. He can sit in his jail cell feeling sorry for himself, or he can embrace his current situation and use it for the glory of God. He can take the initiative and rise above his circumstances, or he can shrug his shoulders and conclude that the whole thing is out of his control. In other words, the choice is his as to whether to view this as a burden or a blessing.

Recently, someone shared with me the story of a concert that Itzhak Perlman, the renowned violinist, once gave at the Lincoln Center in New York City. Any of you who have had the privilege of hearing Perlman play can attest to what a gifted musician he is. During this performance, however, something went wrong. Just a few bars into the opening number, one of the strings of his violin broke. It was such a loud snap that the entire audience immediately realized what had taken place, and they all expected the concert to stop so that he could be brought another violin.

Instead Perlman closed his eyes, waited a moment, and then signaled to the conductor that he wished to continue. Understandably, the orchestra was somewhat apprehensive at first. After all, everyone knows that you cannot perform a major symphonic work with just three strings. You know that, and I know that. But on this particular evening, Itzhak Perlman refused to know that. Indeed, he seemed to play with a renewed passion and energy. You could see him modulating the chords and recomposing the piece as he went.

When he had finished he received a standing ovation — not only from the audience, but from the orchestra as well. Perlman smiled, and then raised his bow to quiet everyone. "Sometimes it is the artist's task," he explained, "to see how much music you can still make with what you have left."

I think the Apostle Paul would have been able to appreciate that. In fact, when I read the opening paragraph of this letter, what I hear is a beautiful hymn of grace and gratitude being played from Paul's prison cell. "I give thanks to God every time I remember you, because of your sharing in the gospel with me," he tells the Philippians. "I am confident of this, that the one who began a good work among you will bring it to completion. And my prayer is that your love may overflow with both knowledge and insight, in order to help you determine what is best. In this way you will be pure and blameless, having produced the harvest of righteousness that comes through Jesus Christ for the glory and praise of God" (vv. 3-6, 9-11). Psychologists would call that reframing. Paul calls it faith.

Burden or blessing — who's to say? According to Paul, we do. We get to choose our perspective. We can decide whether to be imprisoned by our circumstances or empowered by them. It all depends on how you look at life.

Advent 3
Philippians 4:4-7

God's Peace Is On Patrol

On the Sunday afternoon following Thanksgiving, when I was in seventh grade, it began to snow. It started slowly and undramatically — much like any number of other snows I had experienced growing up in Detroit. The sky turned the shade of dirty wool and the flakes danced through the wind as in one of those glass balls that you invert. Little by little the sidewalks whitened, and soon the neighborhood was alive with the rasping sound of shovels. Before long the roads were filled and you could no longer see the curb. The few cars that managed to pass by, plowed through the drifts — their spinning tires forming wings of snow.

By evening the storm had intensified. Ferns of frost sprouted at the corners of my bedroom window, and the bushes outside bowed and splayed like miniature bridesmaids overwhelmed by an armful of frozen flowers. Throughout the night it continued, as an army of plows negotiated the streets, scraping holes in my sleep. When I awoke the next morning, the city lay blanketed beneath nearly two feet of snow. In a town known as the Motor City, all traffic ceased. A litany of closings was recited on the television and the front page had a photograph of two people skiing down the middle of Woodward Avenue!

What I remember most was how silent the city had suddenly become. The only sounds were the caroling of bells from a nearby church, the shouts of children enjoying the unexpected extension of their Thanksgiving vacation, and the muffled conversations of neighbors who hadn't spoken all year. Other than that, everything simply stopped. For a few hours at least, it appeared as if the entire world was at peace.

I often think of that scene when I'm having a stressful day, or find myself becoming anxious and worried about something. Do you ever do that — picture a tranquil place in your mind as a way of relaxing? No doubt, we all have our different images.

For some of you, it might be the serenity of a mountain cabin. It's after dinner. You've just watched the sunset and now it's beginning to get dark — that kind of darkness you can only experience out in the woods, where God displays the stars like diamonds on a jeweler's felt. A soft net of moonlight filters down through the pine trees and unfurls across the lake. The atmosphere is so worshipful, it seems as if creation itself is observing vespers. Choirs of insects offer their chants and hymns, while fireflies swim in the foliage, like tiny votive candles on some unseen altar. You join their meditations, gently rocking on the front porch swing. That is peace.

Or maybe for you, it's strolling on the beach. It's early in the morning. Aside from an occasional jogger, you have the beach all to yourself. You walk at the water's edge as the ocean stitches a ribbon of shells into the sand. Further down the shore, a shower of gulls flirt with the surf, and up on the hillside, the tall grass flickers with butterflies. The sun begins its sturdy ascent, painting the dawn with streaks of orange and red, like celebratory streamers thrown from an arriving vessel. As you walk along, the water licks your ankles, and as quickly as you make footprints in the sand, the waves wash up and fill them again. That is peace.

Here's a good one. You wake up and the clock says it's already after eight. "Oh, my goodness," you think, "I'm going to be late for work." You dash to the bathroom, trying to brush your teeth, comb your hair, and get dressed all at the same time. Then suddenly you remember, "It's Saturday! I don't have to go to work today." You crawl back into bed. The sheets are still warm. And you drift blissfully off to sleep. Now I ask you, do I know what peace is or do I not?

I know this — the scenes I've just described for you have nothing to do with the kind of peace referred to here in Philippians. Paul is not writing this letter from the seclusion of a mountain cabin;

he's writing it from the solitude of a prison cell. We're not sure of his exact location — some think Corinth or Ephesus, others suggest Caesarea. But wherever Paul was, he had evidently been there for a while. Luke indicates that his imprisonment dragged on for over two years (Acts 24:27).

And yet, remarkably, Paul speaks of joy and peace. "Rejoice in the Lord always; again I will say, Rejoice," he encourages the Philippians (v. 4). "Do not worry about anything, but in everything by prayer and supplication with thanksgiving let your requests be made known to God. And the peace of God, which surpasses all understanding, will guard your hearts and minds in Christ Jesus" (vv. 6-7). Some of you may be more familiar with the Revised Standard Version of this passage, which says that God's peace "will *keep* your hearts and minds in Christ Jesus." However, in a striking paradox, Paul actually describes peace here with a military term. A more literal translation would be that the peace of God will "stand sentry watch" over your hearts and minds.

You see, in Paul's mind, peace does not mean a time when there is no hardship or hostility. After all, you don't post guards on the city walls just for decoration. A sentry in the watchtower is evidence that the danger of being attacked is very real. It's not the absence of struggle that defines peace for Paul; it's the presence of love. Put another way, it's not strolling on the beach at sunrise; it's being able to walk through a dark valley unafraid — knowing that, with every step, the Almighty walks beside us and before us.

This is why we can truly rejoice, insists Paul, because God's peace is on patrol. Whatever conflicts arise, whatever challenges await, the One who neither slumbers nor sleeps is vigilantly standing guard. That's not to say that we won't ever encounter adversity. There is always the possibility of an unforeseen threat lurking out there in the shadows. Paul is not naïve to such perils. Nor is he endorsing a policy of casual indifference. What he is suggesting is that we no longer have to tiptoe around, wringing our hands and nervously scanning the horizon. We should be alert, yes; but not anxious.

That's advice worth heeding at any time, of course; but it strikes me as particularly relevant today. For many of us, the tragedy of

September 11 continues to be a source of grave concern. And sadly, the likelihood is that there will be more acts of terrorism in the future. Even as I write this, violence is either breaking out or smoldering just under the surface between the United States and Iraq, China and Taiwan, India and Pakistan, and especially between Jews and Arabs in the Middle East. As Christians, we keep praying and working for peace. But one wonders if we'll ever actually see much of it.

Obviously, we will still sing "Joy to the World" this Christmas, and listen attentively as the angels proclaim, "Glory to God in the highest heaven, and on earth peace among those whom he favors" (Luke 2:14). However, given the current state of world affairs, there's no denying how remote and unrealistic those words now sound. It's almost as if they have become things we wish for, but don't honestly believe we'll witness. And therein lies the difficulty. To paraphrase the psalmist, "How can we continue to sing the Lord's song of peace in a land where that concept seems so foreign?" (Psalm 137:4).

I think this passage may provide a clue. Somehow the Apostle Paul found a way to be at peace, even in a situation that was fraught with uncertainty. He had no idea what he would be facing in the days ahead, but he knew he wouldn't face them alone. Regardless of how bleak his outlook may have appeared, Paul remained confident that God was looking out for him. "For I have learned the secret," he later confides to the Philippians, "of being content in any and all circumstances. I know what it is to have a little, and I know what it is to have a lot. I have sat at the banquet table and enjoyed my fill, and I have languished here in a prison cell, subsisting on only meager resources. And it has taught me that I can do all things through him who strengthens me" (Philippians 4:12-13).

In other words, what Paul discovered is that peace is not determined by our external conditions. Just as you can be lonely in a crowd of people, you can feel anxious and afraid, even in the most tranquil of places. And likewise, you can have a sense of calm, no matter how fierce the storms or frightening the situation. It's not our surroundings that make us secure. It's the sure and certain knowledge that whatever may come, God will never let us go. That is the peace which surpasses all understanding — and I might add, all misunderstandings as well.

Several years ago, I flew to Chicago to attend a conference on preaching. We had all been assigned a book to read in preparation for the event, and my plan was to try to finish it on the flight. Unfortunately, what I failed to anticipate was that I would end up sitting beside someone who wanted to talk. Now, usually, I don't mind conversing with a complete stranger. In fact, I've met some interesting people by doing so. But in this case, I needed to work. So, after we exchanged introductions, I immediately buried my nose in the book, as a way of subtly suggesting that I preferred not to be disturbed.

Apparently, he didn't catch the signal. "What are you reading?" he asked.

"It's a book on preaching," I said.

"Are you a preacher?"

"Yes," I replied, trying to keep my answers as short as possible.

"Where at?"

I told him the name of the church, but secretly hoped that it wouldn't spark any further discussion.

"I had an uncle whose next-door neighbor was a preacher," he volunteered.

"Is that so?" I said, lifting the book a little closer to my face.

"No, I take that back," he quickly added. "That's not right. It wasn't his next-door neighbor. It was the fellow who lived across the street."

I honestly didn't know how to respond at that point, so I just politely nodded.

"Is that book any good?" he inquired.

I was tempted to tell him that this one paragraph (which I had now read for the third time) wasn't bad. But better judgment prevailed and I held my tongue.

"You seem kind of fidgety," he observed. "If you ask me, life is too short to be so stressed out. You need to learn how to be more at peace."

Considering that we had just met, I thought it was a rather impertinent comment. However, before I could reply, a flight attendant came down the aisle offering headphones and I leaped at the opportunity.

About a month later, I received a package in the mail with a return address that I didn't recognize. To my surprise, it contained a set of "worry beads" — the ones that you gently twirl in your fingers to relieve the pressures of the day. There was a tiny card, which read "From Dennis." The only problem was that I didn't know anybody by that name. And it wasn't until I turned the card over that the mystery was resolved, because on the back it said, "To someone who needs to be more at peace." It was then that it suddenly hit me: This is from that guy who sat next to me on the flight.

I was grateful for the gift, of course. But I couldn't help thinking, "What am I supposed to do now? Should I send him a thank you note and leave it at that? Or do I need to get him something in return? And if so, what on earth would it be?" After all, we barely knew each other. We had a passing conversation on an airplane. And suddenly, it's as if he wants a relationship with me.

I eventually wrote him back and we started a correspondence. But as I reflected on the incident, it occurred to me that something like that happened at Christmas. You see, from the very beginning, God kept trying to strike up a conversation with us. Only most of the time, we weren't much interested in talking. We were too wrapped up in our own activities. So one night, God sent us this wondrous gift, as a way of saying, "I don't want you to worry about life anymore, because I'm here to share it with you. I'd like for us to have a relationship."

And if we are willing to accept that gift, and enter into such a relationship, then it won't matter what takes place all around us. Even in the most anxious of times — perhaps especially in those times — God will be right here, standing guard and watching over us. That is peace.

Advent 4
Hebrews 10:5-10

The Ultimate Sacrifice

Back during the first week of November, when the stores were busy trying to persuade us suddenly to be in the Christmas spirit, I have to confess that I wasn't quite ready yet. After all, it's hard to think about Christmas, when you still have leftover Halloween candy in the pantry. But now that it's less than a week away, the same excitement that I remember experiencing as a kid has returned again. And I suspect that's the case for many of you as well. Christmas is just around the corner, and most of us can hardly wait! Our homes are festively decorated. We've been baking cookies with the children, and listening to Bing Crosby on the radio. Some of you may even have a few brightly wrapped packages already beneath the tree.

The last thing that any of us are in the mood for this morning is a lot of vague talk about sacrifice and sin offerings. Which is why our scripture lesson probably strikes you as a strange choice for the Sunday before Christmas. It comes from the Epistle to the Hebrews, which is actually a rather curious book in and of itself. As a matter of fact, we're not even sure who wrote it. A number of candidates have been suggested — Apollos, Barnabas, Clement of Rome, to mention a few — but the arguments aren't very convincing, one way or the other. Even less clear is the letter's intended recipient. Most scholars believe that it was addressed to a specific congregation. However, where they were located and what the church was like are anyone's guess.

About the only thing we're fairly certain of is that the so-called Letter to the Hebrews may not be a letter at all — at least not in the customary sense. While it does contain some epistle-like flourishes toward the end, the main body of Hebrews bears the distinctive marks of being an early Christian sermon. It was likely written by the same pastor who helped to establish this church, and then moved on to engage in missionary activities elsewhere. Evidently, though, he has hopes of returning soon (Hebrews 13:19, 23), and that could be the reason he is sending them an advance copy of this sermon.

There's no doubt that he cares deeply about this congregation, and more importantly, that he is worried about them. At times, you can almost hear the desperate urgency in his voice. "Hold fast to the confession of our hope without wavering," he pleads at one point (Hebrews 10:23). "Lift your drooping hands and strengthen your weak knees," he proclaims at another (Hebrews 12:12). Don't give up. Don't give in. Don't shrink back.

Clearly this is a congregation which is struggling. Part of it has to do with some heretical doctrines with which they have become enchanted. But actually, it's not false teachings that are destroying this church. It's fatigue. In a word, they are exhausted. As one commentator observes, "The threat to this congregation is not that they are charging off in the wrong direction; it's that they do not have enough energy to charge off anywhere."[1] Put another way, what we have here is a church that, for whatever reason, has lost its "Amen," and they are simply too worn down and worn out to bother looking for it.

They are tired — tired of worship, tired of Bible study, tired of prayer group, tired of serving in the world, and frankly, tired of struggling to evangelize it. As a result, they are not so much turning away from the faith as they are drifting away. Attendance has fallen off, contributions are down, enthusiasm is waning, and their self-confidence is beginning to erode. When you lose interest in everything around you, it's usually not long before you start thinking that your own life probably isn't worth getting all that excited about either. Being bored to death is just a less dramatic form of suicide.

Of course, this is not an isolated problem. Most of the people who stop by my office and hand me a letter of resignation are suffering from the same thing. It's not that they're angry or disappointed with the church. In fact, when I ask them what went wrong, they can't really put their finger on anything in particular. What they end up describing is more of a dull ache than a sharp pain. The bottom line is that they're tired. Someone from the Christian Education Committee asked them to teach the sixth grade Sunday school; and they were happy to help out. But that was back in 1982 — and they simply can't bear to walk into that classroom one more time. They've been there, done that, and if they got a T-shirt, it's going in the closet!

Even healthy churches are confronted with this, now and then. So it's hardly surprising that the Preacher of Hebrews would find himself dealing with a weary congregation. Every pastor could cite good, faithful members who have been burned out by the church. What is surprising, however, is how the Preacher decides to deal with this problem. He doesn't try to rally the troops with a lot of gimmicks and quick fixes. There is no appeal for a new mission statement or a reorganization of the committee structure. Little interest is shown in developing focus groups, or even in jazzing up the worship service with a few snappy hymns. Faced with a congregation that barely has a pulse, the Preacher of Hebrews launches into a sermon on — of all things — the sacrificial death of Jesus Christ. Moreover, it is an extremely complex sermon, filled with cryptic Old Testament references and steeped in theological abstractions.

For example, consider the passage we just read. What the Preacher is pointing out here is the never-ending and incomplete nature of the old sacrifices versus the once-and-for-all character of the atonement achieved through Christ. The problem, he argues, with the sacrifices offered under the law of the old cult is that they left people still feeling guilty. If the sacrifices had truly cleansed folks of their sins, they wouldn't be obligated to keep coming back. Indeed, the whole Day of Atonement ritual actually did the opposite of what it promised. Rather than healing people, it was constantly harping on them about what sinful, wretched creatures they were.

Unfortunately, this, too, is not an isolated problem. Even though Christianity doesn't officially observe a Day of Atonement, many churches seem to do a far better job of describing sin than they do of declaring grace. Week after week, congregations are told that, once again, they failed to measure up, and God expects much more from them in the future. Obviously, there are times when that should be stated, if for no other reason than a mushy, liquid diet of "Do as you please, God loves you anyway" provides so little spiritual nourishment. However, if people are given the impression that they will *never* meet God's approval — no matter what they do, or how hard they work at it — they inevitably leave the sanctuary feeling defeated. After all, we can't very well absolve ourselves. That's like trying to sit in your own lap. Our only choice is to slink back next Sunday with another basket of good intentions to place upon the altar, or to stay away altogether because we've grown weary of the effort.

But before we shrug our shoulders and conclude that there's nothing more we can do, the Preacher of Hebrews would like to remind us that, actually, there's nothing more we need to do. What the endlessly repeated sacrifices of old could not achieve, Jesus Christ already accomplished in a single sacrifice. "When Christ came into the world," the Preacher explains, "he spoke to God and said, 'Sacrifices you do not want; sin offerings give you no pleasure. What you desire is for your will to be done. Here I am, O God. I have come to do your will' " (vv. 5-7).

In other words, humankind had reached the point where we were so indebted to God that even our most costly sacrifices were always going to come up short. Any attempt to make amends with God would have been too little too late, because the gap between what the Almighty was owed and what we were able to offer was simply too large. And that's when Christ entered the picture. What he was willing to give more than bridged the gap. Indeed, by sacrificing his own body, he literally stepped into the gap and became the bridge.

Think of it this way. When we have been hurt or disappointed by someone else, often the first step toward reconciliation is to view the situation from their perspective. If we can better understand the other person, we're less likely to feel estranged from them. Similarly, when God was wrestling with how to restore a relationship *with* us, God decided that what was needed was a new way of relating *to* us. You see, experientially, God didn't really know what it was like to be tempted by sin, or to be plagued with doubts, or to grow weary of the relentless pressure that life imposes. God had never tossed and turned all night, or had one of those days where nothing goes right. God was safely ensconced away in the heavens — immune to sickness, removed from suffering, and exempt from death.

By choosing to dwell among us, however, God surrendered all of that, in order to discover what it was like to live life on our terms. As the Preacher of Hebrews expresses it, in Jesus Christ, "We have one who in every respect has been tested as we are, yet without sin" (Hebrews 4:15b). Never again would we be able to claim that God was out of touch, or even out of reach. For the first time, we finally had an advocate who understood exactly what we're going through down here — every headache and heartbreak, every fear and frustration — because he went through it himself.

Of course, from God's standpoint, taking on humanity wasn't particularly practical. In fact, it represented a rather significant gamble. Barbara Brown Taylor once wondered what it might have been like when God initially proposed the plan.[2] The way she pictured it, the cabinet of archangels was assembled, and God carefully explained the idea of going to earth as a baby. Not surprisingly, their reaction was one of stunned silence. Finally the senior archangel stepped forward to speak on their behalf.

"That's an interesting approach, God," he said cautiously. "But to be honest, I'm a little worried about it. After all, you know how people treat one another on earth. Going there as one of them would be putting yourself at their mercy. And if things went awry, there would be no escape. If I could make a suggestion, perhaps you might consider becoming a magical baby with special powers. It wouldn't take much — just the power to become invisible, let's say, or to transport yourself to another place if the need arose. The baby idea is a stroke of genius, God; it really is. However, I think it lacks adequate safety features."

The Almighty smiled, and thanked the archangels for their concern. "No, I think I'll just be a regular baby," God announced. "How else can I gain their trust? How will I ever persuade them that I know their lives inside and out, unless I live a life like theirs? I realize that I'm taking a chance here. But you see, that's part of what I want them to know — that I am willing to risk everything for them. That's how much I love them. And I hope, by doing this, I'll get them to love me in return."

Now, obviously, that's just an imaginative story. However, it does underscore the fact that even Christmas involved a sacrifice on God's part. Actually, the more I think about it, maybe this isn't such a strange scripture lesson for the Fourth Sunday of Advent. What the Preacher of Hebrews is arguing is that we no longer need to offer sacrifices. And part of the reason for that is because, in the person of Jesus Christ, God decided to sanctify the world. By choosing to be born here and living among us, the entire earth suddenly became holy ground.

---

1. Thomas Long, *Hebrews* (Louisville: John Knox Press, 1997), p. 3.

2. Barbara Brown Taylor, *Bread of Angels* (Boston: Cowley Press, 1997), p. 34.

**Christmas Eve/Christmas Day
Titus 2:11-14**

Gift-wrapped In Swaddling Cloths

When I was a kid, Christmas Eve was always the longest night of the entire year. I'm sure many of you remember it being that way too. Around the beginning of the month, my brothers and I would start keeping track of how many weeks remained, and then how many days, and finally, on December 24, we would start counting down the hours. It seemed to take forever for morning to arrive.

Of course, now that I've grown up and become the pastor of a church with four Christmas Eve services — it's still the longest night of the year! However, I'm no longer quite as anxious simply to rush through it. On the contrary, I find myself each year experiencing moments where I am filled with such wonder and awe and overwhelming gratitude that I wish I could somehow push the pause button.

And when you think about it, on a holy and silent night long ago, time did stop. Or better yet, time split. Everything that occurred before this night we call B.C., everything afterwards A.D. They are two different times and two very different worlds. Which is why, in a sense, Christmas Eve becomes the eternal *now*, the time between the times. It is a moment that forever connects those very different worlds and makes them one.

But even more profound than that, what we celebrate tonight is the arrival of One whom we call Emmanuel — the God who is with us. In ways that we will never fully comprehend, this tiny babe is *with* us because he's made out of exactly the same stuff we are, and also the same stuff God is, and he would not let go of either. With outstretched hands he held on to both, so that he could bring the two together. The Apostle Paul put it like this: "He it is who gave himself for us that he might redeem us from all iniquity and purify for himself a people of his own who are zealous for good deeds" (v. 14).

That is the message we proclaim, and if it doesn't strike you as being rather shocking — maybe even a little scandalous — then chances are you have not heard the message for what it is. God gave God's self for us. The high and lofty One became for our sakes lowly and helpless. The eternal and infinite One deliberately chose the constraints of time and flesh. The Father of all mercies put himself at our mercy. I know of no other religion bold enough even to entertain that possibility. Indeed, for other faiths, the suggestion that an omnipotent God might appear in such a vulnerable form would be considered sheer foolishness, or worse still, outright blasphemy.

Yet as I was reading the story just now, I didn't notice any of you squirming in your pews with dismay or leaping to your feet in disgust. Perhaps this story has become so familiar to us that we are no longer startled by it. Or maybe in an effort to make it less startling, we tend to overlook its revolutionary nature. Judging from most of the Christmas cards I receive, I'd say that our inclination is to romanticize the story of Jesus' birth. We picture a quaint, rustic stable somewhere out in the countryside. It's filled with well-groomed livestock and bathed in the warm glow of a lantern's light. Gentle Mary is sitting there, seemingly without a care in the world. Joseph stands beside her, one hand resting softly on her shoulder. The cattle are lowing, the poor baby wakes, but little Lord Jesus, no crying he makes.

Now, come on. You might be able to sell that to Hallmark, but may I have a show of hands from all the parents of newborns who "no crying they make"? When my children were infants, they would sometimes cry half the night. (At least that's what my wife told me; I was usually asleep.)

Please don't get the wrong impression. This story is filled with love. All I'm suggesting is that it's not an overly romantic story. It starts out with a census. The entire empire is forced to relocate temporarily so that Augustus can take down names and hand out numbers. But mind you, it's not because he has suddenly decided to conduct a demographic study. Caesar could not have cared less about fair representation in the Roman senate. Registrations had only one purpose and that was to answer the question of whether there were enough soldiers in the army and enough shekels in the treasury. If the final tally didn't meet the emperor's approval, then you can bet that this edict would have been quickly followed by another: Round up the young men and raise everybody's taxes!

We may have pleasant memories of Christmases past, but not so for the people who lived through the first one. If you had asked any of them what they thought about this census, it's not likely they would have responded, "Oh, what happy times those were. We all got to come home for the holidays." Actually, what they would have said, you probably couldn't print on a Christmas card.

This is hardly a story of "deck the halls" and "fa-la-la-la-la." Poor Mary and Joseph can't even find a decent place to stay for the night. As you recall, there was no room for them in the inn. However, if this is Joseph's hometown, have you ever wondered why they would need to be looking for a hotel? Where are all of their friends and relatives? Why is no one willing to receive them?

I don't know for sure, but I'll venture a guess. Perhaps, given the circumstances of this pregnancy, they have been scandalized. Remember they weren't married at the time. The text reports that Joseph went to Bethlehem to be registered with Mary "to whom he was *engaged* and who was expecting a child" (Luke 2:5, emphasis added). Maybe the reason they can't find a room in somebody's home is because they were not welcomed in anybody's home.

Thus, they end up in a barn, of all places, and a feeding trough (which I can't imagine would have been very sanitary) will serve as Jesus' crib. Both Mary and Joseph are cold, probably hungry, and certainly lonely. None of their family and friends even bothers to show up to celebrate the occasion of this new birth. Their only company that evening are a ragged bunch of shepherds who eventually stumble into the stable — unshowered, unshaven, and unannounced. They are filled with all kinds of strange questions about the baby, and even stranger talk about a chorus of angels in the sky.

Mary is said to have pondered these things in her heart, but if you ask me, that's just a subtle way of suggesting that she didn't have a clue as to what to make of any of this. And of course, neither did Joseph. Once the shepherds depart, they are left to sort it all out by themselves. Even heaven falls silent. There are no anthems of divine assurance that drift sweetly down from above. No angels are sent to attend to their needs, or offer them supportive words of encouragement. You would think that Gabriel — the winged obstetrician who had talked them both into this — could have at least made a follow-up visit to tell them what to do next. But he and all of his celestial cohorts are conspicuously absent. The closing scene of this story is Mary and Joseph sitting alone with their baby, shivering in the night and trying their best to ignore the stench of the animals. It's not exactly Norman Rockwell, is it?

I hope I'm not spoiling your image of Christmas. However, the point is that even in the worst of times, even in the most unimaginable of conditions, God is still present. "For the grace of God has appeared," Paul tells Titus, "bringing salvation to all ..." (v. 11). That is the Good News we declare to the world tonight, and what is both Good and New about it is the incredible claim that, in Jesus Christ, we encounter this grace in person. Emmanuel means God-With-Us, not God-Somewhere-Up-There. Jesus is not a Christmas card from God that says, "Wishing I was there." Jesus is God's way of saying, "I choose to make your home my own."

It reminds me of an experience my wife and I had some years ago with our eldest daughter. Kathy struggled with colic as an infant and often had trouble going to sleep — or more precisely, she had trouble *staying* asleep. She was fine as long as she was in our arms, but as soon as we laid her down she would start screaming. Being first-time parents and not knowing any better, we would naïvely rush to the crib, pick her up, and the whole exhausting cycle would begin again.

I remember one Saturday evening in particular, when I still needed to finish my sermon and little Kathy was not cooperating. My wife and I tried everything. We took turns holding her, rocking her, singing to her. At one point, I even preached my half-written sermon to her. (I figured that if it puts folks to sleep on Sunday morning, it ought to do the trick on Saturday night.) But it was to no avail. Finally, in desperation, I handed Kathy to my wife and said, "I'm sorry, but I've got to get some work done."

I sat down at my computer and started to type. The crying continued incessantly from the other room, and I could tell that my wife wasn't having much success. However, minutes later, the house grew suddenly quiet. I thought to myself, *Will wonders never cease? How did she put that child to sleep? This I've got to see!*

I tiptoed back to the bedroom to witness the miracle firsthand, and what I discovered was that my wife had crawled into the crib *with* Kathy. In effect, she decided to make our child's home her own. It was a humorous sight, I must admit, but as I watched the two of them, it struck me that that's not a bad image for Christmas. On a holy and silent night long ago, God came down from heaven and crawled into the crib of humankind. Only in this case, God took the unprecedented step of actually becoming the child in that crib.

According to Paul, God did this in order to "purify for himself a people of his own who are zealous for good deeds" (v. 14b). In other words, by becoming a baby, God did more than simply make a home among us; God also placed a claim upon us. And if you have ever cradled a newborn in your arms, then I suspect you know exactly what Paul is getting at. There is nothing quite so fragile, so delicate, so vulnerable and utterly dependent as an infant. Which is precisely why an infant summons something from us. During those first precious moments, as a baby begins to take in all the wondrous sights and sounds of life, we can't help but be taken in too. No one remains neutral in a maternity ward. A response is demanded. This tiny, helpless child is reaching up to us for warmth and protection, comfort and nourishment, and above all else, love.

That's part of what makes Christmas Eve so wondrous. For the rest of the year, we will speak of *our* need for God. But not tonight. Tonight we speak of God's need for us — as shocking and scandalous as that may sound! In the worst of times and in the most unimaginable of conditions, God still chose to be with us. And even now, God is reaching up to us with outstretched hands. Because of all places, it is our lives that God has decided to call home tonight.

Christmas 1
Colossians 3:12-17

Forgiveness

In his book *What's So Amazing About Grace?* Philip Yancey tells of a conversation he once had with two scientists who had just emerged from the biosphere near Tucson, Arizona.[1] For those of you who aren't familiar with what that is — several years ago, an isolation experiment was conducted, in which a team of four men and four women lived inside a glass-enclosed structure, entirely shut off from the outer world. The general idea was to see if humankind might one day be able to exist on another planet by recreating a portion of the earth. Consequently, the scientists were expected to be self-reliant, producing everything they would need for survival — including their own oxygen.

Within the biosphere, they had access to fields and forests, jungles and deserts. There was even an ocean (on a much smaller scale, of course). I guess you could think of it as a second attempt at the Garden of Eden. And actually, that may not be such a bad analogy, because they ended up encountering some of the same difficulties that Adam and Eve ran into the first time around. What these scientists admitted to Yancey is that, within a matter of months, the team had splintered into two factions. A minor misunderstanding led to mistrust, which quickly spiraled into accusations of misconduct, and before long, the two groups weren't even speaking. Eventually, the situation became so tense that the experiment had to be called off. In the final report, it was concluded that unless we learn how to forgive each other, it's not likely that we'll survive on this planet much less any other.

One of the guiding principles of economics is that when demand is high and supply low, value increases. If you ask me, that ought to make forgiveness the most precious commodity in the world. I recently heard, for example, of an Apology Sound-Off Line, operated by an organization in Southern California. From what I was able to gather, it offers callers the chance to confess their wrongdoing and express contrition — albeit to an answering machine. And while that may strike you as being rather artificial, apparently business is booming. The service receives an average of 200 calls a day, seven days a week.

Obviously, the demand for forgiveness is exceedingly high. As Paul reminded the Romans, "All have sinned and fall short of the glory of God" (Romans 3:23). That being the case, you would think we'd be doing a better job on the supply side of the equation, by extending forgiveness to one another. After all, if practice makes perfect, this is certainly an area where we're given plenty of opportunities to practice. But you know as well as I, that it's not that simple. Somehow, turning the other cheek has come to mean looking the other way, which is liable to give the impression that we're ignoring the offense or, worse yet, condoning it. Despite hundreds of thousands of sermons on the subject down through the centuries, most of us still find forgiveness to be awkward, painful, and in a word — difficult.

Indeed, at times, it doesn't even feel natural. And maybe that's because it isn't! Like it or not, we live in a world that is very ungracious. It's dog-eat-dog out there, not dog-forgive-dog. Society seems insistent on forever pointing out our shortcomings. When exam papers are handed back in school, it's never the correct answers that are highlighted, only the mistakes. When advertisers make their sales pitch on television, invariably the message is that something is lacking in our lives. We're not popular enough, or powerful enough, or prosperous enough. It's no wonder we are so quick to find fault with one another — that's precisely where we're all taught to focus.

But even more troublesome is the fact that unilateral forgiveness often strikes us as being blatantly unfair. No one wants to be taken advantage of, and excusing a grievous wrong simply because the other person happens to stammer out the words, "I'm sorry," tends to make us feel weak and capitulant, like some mousy Caspar Milquetoast, who is always being pushed around. As a result, whenever we've been injured, we can usually come up with a host of what we think are perfectly legitimate reasons for standing our ground. *They need to learn a lesson,* we'll say. *Letting them off the hook now will only encourage more irresponsible behavior in the future. I'm the one who was hurt here — it's not up to me to make the first move.*

Let's face it. Unconditional forgiveness is not just a difficult act to embrace; it's a hard concept even to swallow. Which is why we may flinch a bit when we hear a scripture passage like this one. Notice that Paul doesn't mention that the other person is remorseful or repentant. He simply says, "Bear with one another and, if anyone has a complaint against another, forgive each other" (v. 13a). Easier said than done, to be sure. But then again, Paul never claims that it will be easy. Nor does he promise that it will be completely satisfying. He knows that the nagging memory of the offense still remains, and that when the wounds run deep, the healing will be slow. The reason he keeps preaching forgiveness is not because it's easy, but because it is essential for our survival. And I'd like to offer a few observations as to why this is the case.

The first is theological; the other two more practical. When it comes to forgiveness, most of us believe that a mere apology without any further consequences just doesn't cut it. Frankly, that's part of what continues to baffle us about grace. It goes against the intuitive sense we all possess that, in the face of a heinous crime, the guilty party cannot be allowed to walk away unpunished. We may debate the appropriate level of that punishment and the means by which it is applied. However, we all agree that, one way or another, a price must be paid. The Apostle Paul wholeheartedly concurs. Only the way he sees it, the price has already been paid — by Jesus Christ. On the cross, God offered up the only Son rather than give up on all of us.

Some of you may be remember the movie *The Last Emperor*, which tells the story of the young boy who became the final emperor of China, prior to the Communist revolution. As you might imagine, he lived a life of luxurious splendor, surrounded by a multitude of servants ready to fulfill his every desire. At one point in the film, his brother ventures the question, "What happens when you misbehave?" Giggling with delight, the boy emperor explains, "Someone else gets punished." His brother is skeptical. So the boy emperor breaks a nearby vase, and sure enough, one of the servants is promptly beaten. According to Paul, just the opposite happened with Christ. The servants misbehaved, and the King was punished.

Exactly how this resulted in our being forgiven is a mystery we will never fully comprehend. Paul readily admits that the cross seems absurd to some, and abhorrent to others. But there's no denying that it cost God something very dear, and that's precisely why Paul is so insistent that we forgive each other. "Just as the Lord has forgiven you," he tells the Colossians, "so you also must forgive" (v. 13b). He's not suggesting that God will forgive us only to the extent that we forgive others. If God's forgiveness operated under those conditions, we couldn't very well call it grace. What Paul is saying is that if we can't open our hearts to those around us, then our hearts are likely to remain closed to God as well. In other words, the same stubborn pride that keeps us from extending forgiveness may also keep us from experiencing it. We have to be willing to reach out in order to reach up.

My second observation concerning forgiveness is that, given the alternatives, it's the one thing that truly works. The other options, of course, are resentment and revenge — neither of which offers an escape from the pain that we're dealing with in the first place. In fact, our word "resentment" literally means "to feel again." It's like picking at a scab. The wound never heals, because we never allow it to. We keep reliving the event in our minds, traveling back to the source of the suffering and being hurt by it all over again. However, since none of us can change the past, why would we want to remain imprisoned there?

Revenge is likewise a trap — only instead of imprisoning us in the past, it locks us into a future of forever trying to even the score. And therein lies the primary flaw with the law of revenge. It never gets what it's after. Fairness and parity are never achieved. On the contrary, it ties the injured and injurer together in a never-ending cycle, which usually spins out of the control of both and takes on a life of it own. The taste of revenge may seem sweet, but when dinner is served, we're the ones who end up being eaten alive. That's why it's called an all-consuming passion.

Forgiveness is a way to be released from the self-inflicted punishment of resentment and the self-destructive path of revenge. It's not an easy way out. We don't automatically forget the wrong that was done to us. But at least we're now free to move forward, because it's no longer setting the agenda for our lives.

Which brings me to my final observation: Often the person who is most healed by forgiveness is the one actually doing the forgiving. Frederick Buechner put it like this, "When somebody you've wronged forgives you, you're spared the dull and self-diminishing throb of a guilty conscience. When you forgive somebody who has wronged you, you're spared the dismal corrosion of bitterness and wounded pride. For both parties, forgiveness means the freedom again to be at peace inside their own skin and to be glad in each other's presence."[2]

Several years ago, a fifth-grade boy named Jacob was killed just a few blocks from the church. He was riding his bike, lost his balance, and fell in front of a passing car. There were no charges filed, because the accident was deemed unavoidable. However, the tragedy was compounded by the fact that the driver was a high school student.

Since Jacob's family had no church of their own, I went to the house the following day and offered the use of our sanctuary for a memorial service. Needless to say, it was a very emotional meeting. We wept together over what had happened, and wondered together about what might have been and now never would. Their desire was for the service to be a celebration of Jacob's life. "He was such a happy child," his mother explained, "that I can't imagine having one of those dreary, somber funerals. It just wouldn't be right."

His father asked if he could have a moment to speak during the service. My initial impression was that he simply wanted to share some personal thoughts, and to thank the community for the outpouring of support that the family had received. However, when he came forward, he brought with him a small potted plant. He talked of the pain that he had been dealing with, and the wide range of emotions he continued to experience. "They say that time heals all wounds," he observed, "but I can't wait that long. I need to begin the healing process now. There is a young man here this morning who is hurting every bit as much as we are."

Jacob's father walked out into the sanctuary carrying the plant and presented it to the driver of the car which had killed his son. The two embraced, and between tears, briefly spoke. I have no idea what was said, but as far as I'm concerned, the sermon that day had already been preached. It was an act of such courage and compassion that a lot of us didn't want to leave the church, even after the service was over. It was as if we had witnessed something very precious — something we all yearn for, but that the world doesn't supply very often. Forgiveness. It's not easy, of course. Nor do we suddenly stop hurting once we forgive. However, it is the surest way to survive the pain, and ultimately, to be set free from it.

---

1. Philip Yancey, *What's So Amazing About Grace?* (Grand Rapids: Zondervan Publishing, 1997), p. 83.

2. Frederick Buechner, *Wishful Thinking: A Theological ABC* (New York: Harper & Row, Publishers), p. 29.

Christmas 2
Ephesians 1:3-14

God's Benefactors

Once when I returned home for a quick visit with my parents, an old friend unexpectedly dropped by to see me. We took advantage of the warm spring weather and sat out on the back porch. A tiny cluster of maple trees exhaled the fragrance of sticky new buds, as Fred and I reminisced about our high school days and exchanged the latest gossip concerning classmates. It wasn't long, though, before we found ourselves running out of things to say. Like trying to read the comic strips after returning from an extended vacation, we had lost the continuity of each other's stories.

After an awkward pause, Fred fished a pack of cigarettes from his pocket. I noticed that he had taken to wearing a perpetual squint — either from needing glasses, or smoking too much, or simply because he wasn't able to look at the world wide-eyed anymore. He seemed on the verge of confessing something. But he let the moment pass and gazed out at the forsythia bushes, which swayed back and forth in the breeze like a dancing yellow fog.

"How have you been?" I finally asked.

"Fa-air," he said hesitantly, dragging the word into two syllables.

"Do you want to talk about it?"

"I'm not even sure where to begin," he admitted, stabbing a cigarette into his mouth. "I've been kind of depressed these last few months. But it's like one of those equations we used to have in algebra class with nothing but variables; I can't seem to solve it."

I tried to gauge my response carefully, sensing that our conversation had now moved from a thick deceptive forest to more of a desert where my every step would leave a print. "I'd be willing to listen," I said.

He trailed his fingers cautiously along the table, as if searching for an entry point to the discussion. "I don't want to give you the wrong impression," he explained. "I have a pretty good life. I enjoy my work, I meet a lot of fascinating people, and I do a lot of interesting things. Except lately, for some reason, it all seems scattered and disconnected — like pearls without a string."

I was about to weigh in with an observation, but he suddenly went on with a staccato burst of candor. "I think my problem is that I'm not committed to anything. There is no person, no organization, no principle or cause to which I am a hundred percent committed. I have all these ties, but none of them are binding." He leaned back in his chair and dismissed a plume of smoke, "Do you suppose that might be it?"

Having recently completed a building campaign at the church, I was immediately tempted to launch into one of my ready-to-preach commitment sermons. What I was going to say to him was something along these lines. *You had better believe that's the reason you're so depressed. How can you possibly expect your life to have any meaning or value or purpose, unless you're committed to something? Now pull yourself together, and go out there and get involved!*

That was the advice I was prepared to offer. However, there was something about the way the cigarette kept trembling in Fred's hand, as the smoke bled slowly through his fingers, which silenced my sermonic impulse. And I now think it was one of those grace-filled occasions when the Holy Spirit provided me with the right words, because what I ended up saying was: "You tell me that you're not committed to anything or anyone. But I wonder if the real issue is that you don't honestly believe that there is anyone who is committed to *you*?"

Tears began to percolate in his eyes. "You know, it is sheer hell," he whispered, "when you don't feel like you belong."

Have any of you ever experienced that feeling? Have you ever struggled with the sense that you don't belong anywhere — I mean, *really* belong? It's one thing to be part of a group where everybody shares a common interest. But it's another thing altogether to know that someone out there is interested in you. I've met people who are members of a dozen different organizations, and involved in activities morning, noon, and night, and they still seem to carry around this emptiness deep inside. It's almost as if they realize that something is missing in their life, but they're not sure what. And worse yet, they secretly suspect that if *they* were ever missing, no one would even notice.

No doubt, we have all felt like that at one time or another, which is why I hope you were listening closely as the scripture lesson was being read just now. Judging by the way that the letter to the Ephesians starts out, Christianity is more than our making a commitment to God; it's also the recognition that God has made a significant commitment to us. In fact, according to Paul, this commitment began before we were even born. In the person of Jesus Christ, God chose us "before the foundation of the world to be holy and blameless" (v. 4). The Almighty "destined us for adoption as children" (v. 5). Paul goes on to affirm that "in Christ we have obtained an inheritance ... so that we, who were the first to set our hope on Christ, might live for the praise of his glory" (vv. 11-12).

In effect, this opening passage is like the reading of a will, in which we are all listed as God's benefactors. I don't know how many of you have ever been to the reading of a will. But I assume that even if you haven't, you have a vague idea of what happens at one. Typically, the family and relatives, as well as anybody else who expects to be involved in the distribution of the estate, gather together in a lawyer's office and wait for their names to be called. It can be a very exciting time for some, and I'm guessing, a very anxious time for others. After all, you don't want to show up if your name is not going to be mentioned. It would be rather humiliating to find out at that point that you didn't really belong.

And yet, within the history of ancient Israel, there were some folks who didn't need to be present when the will was read. They might as well have stayed at home, because their names would never be called. For starters, the widow didn't need to be there. Strange as it may seem to us, the law dictated that she was not to inherit a thing. She was a woman, and in those days, property was handed down strictly through men. It was father to son, uncle to nephew, brother to brother.

If you were a slave, you also didn't need to bother showing up. Your name might have been called, but it was more in terms of who was going to inherit you, not what you were going to inherit. Slaves were part of the estate, never the benefactors thereof. Likewise, if you were a foreigner, you could safely skip the reading of the will. Your name wouldn't be on the list. People who were not children of Israel were widely regarded as nobodies. They may have lived there, but in the eyes of the law, they didn't belong there, and so they got nothing.

That's just the way it was. Some folks were in; others were out. But then again, are things really that different today? The world is still largely made up of the haves and the have-nots. There are some who own vacation homes on three continents, and others who sleep each night on a park bench beneath a blanket of newsprint. There are some whose pantries and tables are laden with food, and others whose stomachs go empty. There are some who can't figure out which party to attend this weekend, and others who will sit in their apartments all alone. That's just the way it is.

But according to the Bible, that's not the way it will always be. The future is not merely an endless extension of the status quo. God is the One who holds the future, and God's future has a way of surprising and disrupting human expectations. In Isaiah 56, for example, there is a marvelous passage where the Lord says, "I do not want foreigners to say, 'I do not have a place among the people of God.' I do not want the eunuch to say, 'I am just a dead tree.' The day is coming," says the Lord, "when the stranger, the alien, the foreigner, the transient will all have a place in my house. And those who find themselves without children will have better than sons and daughters, because I will put their name on a marker in my house and everybody will know them forever. That day is coming," says Isaiah, "when God's house shall be called a house of prayer for everybody" (Isaiah 56:3-8).

Thomas Long tells the story of a faculty colleague, who once arrived at the airport early for a flight and decided to pass the time by grading papers in one of the waiting areas. His seat happened to be directly opposite a restaurant, and as he worked, he noticed that the restaurant was empty except for one man, who was sitting idly in the corner, with his head resting on the tabletop. It was obvious from his dress that he was one of the homeless folk who had taken up residence in the airport, and it was equally obvious from his manner that he was not in the restaurant as a paying customer.

After a few minutes, another man who seemed to be the restaurant manager walked firmly and swiftly toward the homeless man. It appeared as if a scene was about to develop, in which the manager was going to ask this street person to leave the premises. Surprisingly, though, as the manager walked by the table, he put a hot dog in front of the man. On the way back, he placed a cup of coffee beside the hot dog.

Thomas Long notes that, on the one hand, you could view this as a simple act of human kindness, somebody giving food to a hungry person. From another perspective, however, you could also see it as a glimpse into God's future — a prophetic act that looked toward the day when everyone will sense that they are part of the family. Because when the manager gave this man some food and drink, not stopping to receive praise or to make the man feel like some debtor, what he said in essence was this. *Friend, in a little while, I'm going to have to pretend that my main identity is as a restaurant manager and that your main identity is as a homeless trespasser, and I'm going to have to tell you that you don't belong here. That's just the way things are, right now. But, at least for a moment, let us assume the identities that we will surely have in the future of God. Here you are, brother, welcome to the joyful feast.*[1]

In other words, in God's future, there will no longer be the haves and the have-nots. There will no longer be those whose names are called, and those who wait in vain for someone to notice them. There will no longer be people who are left out or overlooked. For we will all be brought together in God's house, and made to feel that we truly belong there. That day is coming, say the prophets. And what Paul wants to point out is that, in the person of Jesus Christ, that day arrived! The way he put it, when we first heard the gospel and believed in Christ, "We were marked with the seal of the promised Holy Spirit; this is the pledge of our inheritance toward redemption as God's own people" (vv. 13-14).

Some time ago, I heard about a reporter who had toured the country interviewing the elderly about their earliest experiences. One of the people he happened to encounter was a man by the name of Bernum Ledford. He was a hundred-and-something years old, living in a nursing home in Kentucky, and he remembered as a child being introduced to his great-great-grandmother.

"What was it like meeting her?" this reporter asked. With a soft smile, Bernum said, "I'll never forget that day. It was a hot, humid Sunday afternoon, and it was a long trip. I had never met her before, and I wasn't real excited about going all that way just to see some old woman. To make matters worse, when we finally got to her house and went inside, I saw that not only was she old but blind, and not only blind but actually kind of mean looking. And so, at first, I was afraid of her.

" 'We brought Bernum along to see you,' my father said. She turned in my direction with outstretched arms and long, bony fingers, and said, 'Bring him over here.'

"They practically had to push me across the room," Bernum told the reporter, with a chuckle. "But when I eventually got there, I found that those same hands, which I been so frightened by, were surprisingly gentle. She carefully traced the outline of my face, and ran her fingers through my hair. And then, in a voice filled with love and acceptance, I heard her whisper: 'This boy is one of ours. This boy is part of our family. This one belongs to us.' "

I believe that what Paul is saying in this passage is that before we were first introduced to God — or for that matter, before even the foundation of the world — God's gentle hands reached out and chose us to be benefactors, the inheritors of the glory of Christ. In fact, if you listen closely to these verses, you can still hear the merciful whispers of the Almighty: "These ones are my children. These ones are part of my family. These ones belong to me."

---

1. Thomas G. Long, "Preaching God's Future: The Eschatological Context of Christian Proclamation," in *Sharing Heaven's Music*, ed. by Barry L. Callen (Nashville: Abingdon Press, 1995), pp. 201-202.

**Epiphany 1
(Baptism Of The Lord)
Acts 8:14-17**

Crossing Borders And Breaking Down Boundaries

Luke reports this story in such an understated and matter-of-fact style that one could easily miss the significance of what is being described here. In the space of four brief verses, we're told that Peter and John are sent on behalf of the apostles in Jerusalem to pray over and lay their hands upon some recent converts to Christianity. But mind you, they are doing this in Samaria, of all places. That's not only remarkable; it's nothing short of revolutionary.

As you no doubt recall, there was a long history of enmity between the Jews and the Samaritans. It all started back in the eighth century B.C., when the Assyrians invaded the Northern Kingdom. As conquerors were wont to do in those days, they proceeded to transport the brightest and best of the population away. Basically, the only folks they left were the ones they had little use for — the poor, the less educated, and the unskilled. Eventually, these people began to intermarry with the strangers that the Assyrians had settled in their land, and the result was an entirely new race, the Samaritans.

In the sixth century B.C., a similar fate befell the Southern Kingdom. The Babylonians invaded, conquered, and carried off the brightest and best from that country. However, they stubbornly refused to lose their identity. Intermarriage was strictly forbidden, in order to keep the Jewish bloodline pure. When they were allowed to return in the fifth century B.C., and began to rebuild Jerusalem under the leadership of Ezra and Nehemiah, the Samaritans from the Northern Kingdom offered to help. But by this time, they were considered a mixed breed — impure and inferior. Thus, the

Jews wanted nothing to do with them. From that day onward there remained an unhealed breach and a bitter hatred between the two races.

You pick a lot of this up in the Gospels, of course. When Jesus' critics wish to insult him, for instance, they call him "a Samaritan" (John 8:48). When Jesus is talking with the Samaritan woman at the well (something that surprised even his disciples), John carefully notes that "Jews do not share things in common with Samaritans" (John 4:9), the implication being that, ordinarily, these two groups did not speak to one another, much less interact. They did whatever was necessary to avoid contact, even if it meant traveling miles out of their way. In fact, in Matthew's Gospel, when Jesus sends the disciples out as missionaries, he initially tells them, "Go nowhere among the Gentiles, and enter no town of the Samaritans" (Matthew 10:5).

And yet, here in this passage, Peter and John are specifically sent to Samaria, in order to welcome these people into the Christian community. According to Luke, they "went down and prayed for them that they might receive the Holy Spirit" (v. 15). But if you ask me, the Holy Spirit was already there, because it had been the Spirit that prompted Philip to preach the gospel to the Samaritans in the first place. You see, the dangerous thing about the Holy Spirit is that one can never be sure where it will lead you or even to whom it will lead you. Jesus said it was like the wind. "The wind blows where it chooses, and you hear the sound of it, but you do not know where it comes from or where it goes. So it is with everyone who is born of the Spirit" (John 3:8).

Simply put, the Holy Spirit is not restricted by national borders or racial boundaries. It pays no attention whatsoever to the arbitrary distinctions that we seem to draw among ourselves. Just as God makes the sun shine on the good and evil alike and sends rain upon both the righteous and the unrighteous, so, too, does the wind of the Spirit sweep across the land, whether it be inhabited by Jew or Samaritan. As far as I can tell, there is nothing you can do to plan for the Spirit or even to predict whether it will blow into your life like a gentle breeze or a window-rattling squall. About the best you can do is be willing to move when it does and not be too choosy about where it ends up taking you, since you're not the one doing the choosing.

Judging by this passage, however, one of the trademarks of the Holy Spirit is to give people a way back into relationship with each other. Maybe something like this has even happened to you. For example, if you have ever found yourself being moved toward reconciliation with someone to whom you had previously been estranged or offering a word of forgiveness that you had not originally planned to offer — if you have ever found yourself taking a risk that you didn't think you had the courage to take or reaching out to someone you had intended to walk away from — then chances are you were being carried in that direction by the winds of the Holy Spirit. But just in case you're wondering, here's how you can tell for sure. If it felt like a fresh breeze just blew down the cluttered corridors of your life, blasting open locked doors and setting you free, then it's a pretty safe bet that the Spirit was at work. I dare say, Peter and John must have felt that way when they suddenly found themselves laying hands on the very people with whom they wouldn't even have shaken hands before.

I don't know how many of you are familiar with a man named Edward Lorenz. He is best known for his contributions in the area of physics. However, that's not actually how he began his career. He was a research meteorologist at the Massachusetts Institute of Technology in the early 1960s. The project he happened to be working on was mapping out weather patterns. The way he figured it, if astronomers can look 76 years into the future and accurately tell us when Haley's Comet will return, he ought to be able to predict the weather a month from now. He just needed to determine all of the variables and come up with a system that would help him chart it out.

He was working on a Royal McBee computer, which, by today's standards, probably chugged along about as fast as a small riding mower. But it was perfectly able to perform the kind of calculations that he required. What Lorenz did was to observe how weather patterns changed over the course of time. Based on this research, he came up with a dozen mathematical formulas defining the relationship between air temperature and barometric pressure, between pressure and wind speed, and so forth. He plugged them all into his computer and let the systems fly. Piles and piles of printouts stacked up around his office, each one detailing the development of a particular weather pattern.

The only problem was that he could never make these patterns repeat themselves. There were similarities, but never exact duplication. Even when he plugged in the same variables, they always seemed to produce a different result. That puzzled Lorenz, because, in effect, he had constructed an artificial universe here on his computer. All of the rules that governed these weather patterns were fixed. They weren't being influenced by any other factors. Thus, one would think that you should be able to arrive at a predictable outcome. But no matter how often he tried, Lorenz could never make the weather patterns do what they were supposed to.

Finally, one winter day in 1961, he decided to take a shortcut. He wanted to look at one part of a particular sequence in more detail, but he didn't want to start the whole run over again from the beginning. So he started it in the middle instead, giving the pattern its initial conditions by typing the numbers straight from an earlier printout. Then he went down the hall for a cup of coffee.

When he returned, Lorenz found a weather pattern so different from the previous one that there was simply no resemblance between the two. He checked his numbers. He checked the vacuum tubes in the computer. Then he realized what had happened. One of the numbers he was working with was .506127. To save space, he had rounded it off to .506, thinking a difference of .000127 was inconsequential. After all, in a vast weather system, a number that small would be like a baby's sneeze, or perhaps the beat of a butterfly's wings. However, as Lorenz had just learned, even that tiny number, way down there in the hundred-thousandths, turned out to be the difference between a gentle rain shower and a monsoon.

His discovery was the beginning of a new branch of science, which we know today as "the theory of chaos." Chaos theory teaches us that a tiny, seemingly inconsequential difference at one point in a system changes the whole system. It's almost as if the entire universe is connected, woven together in a single fabric, and a change anywhere else in the universe affects the whole. What

Lorenz eventually concluded from this is that not only we will never be able to predict the weather — at least not exactly — we're not going to be able to predict much of anything else either. There are simply too many variables. Everything happening in the universe affects everything else. That's why life tends to be rather chaotic (which, of course, you don't have to be a physicist to verify). There is an essential messiness and randomness to life that cannot be controlled, no matter how hard we try. That's the bad news about chaos theory.

Here's the good news. Apparently, there's a boundary to it. Because what Edward Lorenz discovered on his good, old trusty Royal McBee computer and what scores of scientists after him later confirmed is that even though chaotic systems never behave the same way twice and are therefore unpredictable, there is an outer limit beyond which they will not go. In other words, while it's true that Lorenz could never get his weather systems to repeat themselves, he couldn't push them into total chaos either. There was this mysterious force, Lorenz concluded, that kept pulling at the chaos and forming it into patterns.

Lorenz and his colleagues decided to name this force "the strange attractor," since that's precisely what it seemed to be doing — attracting and arranging the chaos.[1] The Bible, of course, has a different name for this force: the Holy Spirit. Way back at the very beginning, the book of Genesis tells us, the Spirit of God moved across the face of the chaos and began shaping it into order (Genesis 1:1-2). And that Spirit has never stopped moving. It keeps pulling at us and pushing us in new and surprising directions.

Peter and John found that out firsthand. For centuries, the relationship between Jew and Samaritan resembled little more than chaotic estrangement. The only thing that seemed predictable was that these two groups couldn't stand being together, much less coming together. That is, until the winds of the Holy Spirit swept in, like an unpredictable change in the weather, and brought them together.

---

1. Barbara Brown Taylor, *The Luminous Web: Essays on Science and Religion* (Cambridge: Cowley Press, 2000), pp. 93-96.

**Epiphany 2
Ordinary Time 2
1 Corinthians 12:1-11**

The Multitasking Church

For the next six Sundays we will be looking at passages from the concluding chapters of the First Letter to the Corinthians. That being the case, I thought it worthwhile to give you a little background on the circumstances that prompted Paul to write this epistle.

One needs only to consider the geography of Greece to appreciate why Corinth was destined to become the commercial capital of the Mediterranean. Situated on a narrow isthmus, the city literally bridged northern Greece with the southern Peloponnesian peninsula, and because the isthmus was just four miles across from sea to shining sea, it was also easily accessible to both the Adriatic and the Aegean. As a result, almost everything that could be bought, sold, or traded eventually made its way through there. A quick trip to the market, for example, would allow you the opportunity to sample Phoenician dates, or barter for Libyan ivory, or check out an authentic Cilician goats' hair blanket. In effect, Corinth was where the ancient world went shopping.

Unfortunately, exotic merchandise wasn't the only thing being offered at bargain basement prices. It was widely held that moral standards and common decency had been drastically discounted as well. Ever since the time of Aristophanes, the city claimed the rare distinction of actually having its name turned into a verb. To "corinthianize" was a slang term which meant "to go to the dogs" — presumably because it was wild, ravenous beasts that would most feel at home there.

The population was largely immigrant, as merchants and mariners drifted in from all directions, toting their foreign gods along with them — Artemis from Ephesus, Astarte from Syria, Iris and Seraphis from Egypt. There was a veritable smorgasbord of deities to choose from, and towering above them all, perched atop a summit known as Acrocorinth, stood a temple dedicated to the love goddess Aphrodite. It was said to have been frequented by over 1,000 sacred prostitutes and no telling how many lustful worshipers. In a sense, though, the temple epitomized what the city itself had become — a town where pretty much everything was for sale.

It would be difficult to imagine a more unlikely location for a New Church Development. Indeed, one of the common proverbs in those days was, "Not everybody should go to Corinth!" And there were probably times when Paul wished he'd taken that advice to heart. He arrived around 50 A.D., following a rather disappointing stint in Athens, where most folks simply laughed at his absurd babbling about a man risen from the dead. Why he happened to select Corinth as his next stop is anyone's guess. But then again, perhaps Paul figured that in a city willing to buy just about anything, his message stood a better chance of being received.

At any rate, he wound up staying with a couple named Priscilla and Aquilla, who had fled to Corinth after Emperor Claudius decided to clear all the Jews out of Rome. We're not exactly sure how Paul came to know the two of them. However, since they were tentmakers like him, he may have worked at their shop in exchange for room and board. They soon introduced him to the neighborhood synagogue, and being a distinguished guest, Paul was given the honor of addressing the congregation. He basically delivered the same sermon that he had preached back at the Areopagus. The only difference was that while the Athenians had been amused, the Corinthians were not. They were horrified at Paul's insistence that a relatively unknown Nazarene named Jesus, who had been executed as a seditious criminal some twenty years earlier, was none other than the long-awaited Messiah. To put it bluntly, the suggestion that a crucified felon could somehow be God's chosen One was beyond ludicrous; it was downright blasphemous.

In fact, it created so much controversy that Paul was promptly informed that, not only were they not interested in hearing him again, they didn't particularly care to see him anymore either. He may have been a visitor in those parts, but he had worn out his welcome with them, and in no uncertain terms, he was told to move on. So that's precisely what Paul did — except he didn't end up moving very far. He started a church next door to the synagogue in the house of one Titus Justus, and within a matter of weeks it was already filled with Jewish converts, including a man named Crispus, who had been the synagogue's leading ruler.

Paul worked with them for about a year and a half, preaching the gospel and teaching them the fundamentals of Christian theology. Eventually, though, he felt the call to continue his missionary activities elsewhere and bid the tiny congregation farewell. After a brief stop in the harbor town of Cenchreae, Paul sailed eastward across the Aegean and ultimately settled in Ephesus (just outside of what is today Izmir, Turkey). It was there, a few months later, that he received an anxious letter telling him, in effect, that if he were to return to Corinth he would likely find more than one church. Apparently, they had started to splinter into different denominations, tragically foreshadowing what continues to occur within Christianity even today.

One group followed Paul, another his successor Apollos, still another the Apostle Peter, and yet a fourth group of gnostics rallied around a spiritualized version of Jesus Christ — whom they claimed didn't actually die upon the cross, since he was never a real, flesh-and-blood person in the first place. To complicate matters even further, there were also a number of charismatics who specialized in prophecy and speaking in tongues, and who tended to turn every worship service into either a skills competition or a talent show. One member of the congregation was openly living with his stepmother as husband and wife. Some folks were treating the Lord's Supper with all the dignity of a spring break fraternity party. Others had concluded that the way to attract a more sophisticated clientele was to rule out the resurrection altogether. And on and on it went. Apart from that, things were going just fine!

Paul's response to this whole convoluted mess is what we now know as First Corinthians. Obviously, he was disappointed to learn what had taken place there since his departure. However, he doesn't appear to be terribly interested in analyzing how things could have disintegrated so quickly. What he does instead is to offer them a refresher course in "Christianity 101." In other words, rather than trying to sort out a situation that was already sordid enough, he almost immediately turns his attention to getting them back on track.

One by one, he addresses each of their concerns and even expresses some of his own. He tackles questions about sex and marriage, the proliferation of lawsuits, the role of women in the church, the eating of food dedicated to idols, and the etiquette of celebrating Holy Communion, to name just a few. But while Paul is happy enough to provide his two cents on all of these practical matters, for him there was actually a deeper issue at stake. The real question was not "What must we do?" or even "How should we behave?" but "To whom do we belong?"

Paul makes that clear at the letter's outset. He willingly concedes that, in most respects, the Corinthians were no better than anybody else. In fact, as far as the world was concerned, they were considerably worse. "Not many of you were wise by human standards," he reminds them, "not many were powerful, not many were of noble birth" (1 Corinthians 1:26). All of which was true, of course. This was basically a blue-collar congregation, consisting of slaves, dockhands, artisans, housewives, and what have you. None of them were ever going to be confused with the city's elite and well established. Nor would they have even dreamed of making such a claim.

Nevertheless, what Paul hopes they will keep in mind is that the risen Lord has made a claim upon them. They have been sanctified in Jesus Christ. "Do you not know that you are God's temple and that God's spirit dwells in you?" he asks at one point (1 Corinthians 3:16). Regardless of how the world happened to view them, Paul wants the Corinthians to realize that they are not nobodies; they are somebodies. More precisely, they are Christ's body! Which is why their current behavior strikes him as so unseemly. If this was their idea of being the body of Christ — his eyes, his mouth, his hands — then all they have done is to create the impression that our Savior was blind, tongue-tied, and all thumbs.

But what disturbed Paul even more was their incessant and rather infantile squabbling over spiritual gifts. As we read, he first broaches this issue at the beginning of chapter 12. "I do not want you to be uninformed," he writes. "Therefore I want you to understand that no one speaking by the Spirit of God ever says, 'Let Jesus be cursed!' and no one can say, 'Jesus is Lord,' except by the Holy Spirit" (v. 3). That was the dividing line for Paul; and mind you, it's the *only* one he offers. He doesn't mention any of the categories that so many of today's denominations seem eager to establish — liberal versus conservative, contemporary worship versus traditional, pro-choice versus pro-life, those who desire to change ordination standards versus those who strive for ethical consistency among the clergy.

Please don't get the wrong idea. I'm not trying to minimize these differences. They are very real, and they make the road ahead an extremely perilous one. These are difficult times for the church, to be sure. Many are the controversies, varied are the passions and special interests, diverse are the opinions, and deep is the pain — on all sides! However, what I hear Paul saying in this passage is that going our separate ways is not an acceptable option. Simply put: it's not our decision to make. After all, we didn't choose to be a part of the body; Christ chose us (John 15:16).

The one distinguishing characteristic of Christianity, according to Paul, is the declaration of Jesus Christ as Lord. There may be some who proclaim beliefs that sound un-Christian to you. There may even be some who practice what strike you as blatantly un-Christian behaviors. And in fact, you may be correct in your assessment. But as wrong as those beliefs and behaviors may be, it does not give any of us the right to exclude such ones from the church. If they profess Jesus Christ as their Lord, they are still part of the body.

Of course, this doesn't mean that we should just ignore our differences. Denial doesn't serve truth any more than avoidance solves conflict. Paul is not suggesting that we stop challenging and correcting one another. This entire letter is filled with corrective advice, often stated in the strongest terms possible. What Paul is pointing out, however, is that we can *admonish* our fellow Christians, while at the same time *affirming* them as fellow Christians. As he goes on to explain, "There are varieties of gifts, but the same Spirit; and there are varieties of services, but the same Lord; and there are varieties of activities, but it is the same God who activates all of them in everyone" (vv. 4-5).

The operative word here is "varieties." Most churches do a fairly good job of emphasizing that we all have our unique gifts and abilities. But equally important is the fact that there are different avenues of service and different types of activities. I suppose you could argue that if everyone is doing one's own thing, it's liable to send the church in divergent directions. But then again, just as our own bodies are capable of performing more than one task — such as, let's say, chewing gum and walking at the same time — it seems reasonable to think that the body of Christ is also perfectly able to perform a multitude of complex and even contrary tasks.

Indeed, if the Christian community is to bear witness to all people, it may actually require this kind of variety. Thus, rather than being suspicious or resentful of other Christians who bear their witness in ways different from our own, why should we not be grateful for them? After all, they may be able to do and say things that we cannot and reach people that we haven't yet. Despite our differences, insists Paul, we still affirm fundamentally the same thing — that Jesus Christ is Lord and head of the church.

Fred Craddock once shared an insightful story about the construction of two houses in his neighborhood. In the case of one, he observed that the builder was carefully examining each stone, in order to make sure that they were exactly the same. However, he wasn't using any mortar. He was just placing them one on top of another. Craddock remarked that that was a rather unconventional practice. "What's going to keep those stones together?" he asked. "They're all identical" was the reply.

Meanwhile, across the street, a second builder was making use of the very stones that the first fellow had rejected. His were a hodgepodge assortment of different shapes and sizes. In fact, they didn't even look like they belonged together. "You'll have trouble getting those to stay," Craddock said. "No, I won't," the builder explained, "because I've got something here to hold them in place."

Craddock wondered what it might be. "He didn't call it mortar," Craddock acknowledged. "From what I could tell, it seemed like he referred to it as Christian love. And sure enough, within a matter of days, the first house was rubble, and the other stood tall and proud."

The Apostle Paul seems convinced that if we can faithfully and lovingly continue to serve together, study together, and even struggle together — we ought to be able to stay together. For in so doing, we truly become the church that Christ built upon the solid rock and against which even the fiercest storms of conflict shall never prevail.

**Epiphany 3
Ordinary Time 3
1 Corinthians 12:12-31a**

Not Just Any Body, Christ's Body

Let me offer you a hypothetical situation. Suppose you had a friend who was unfamiliar with the church. The person had never attended a worship service or sat in on a Sunday school class. He or she had never participated in any of the midweek fellowship activities or volunteered to help out with one of the mission trips. In effect, Christianity was a complete mystery to him/her. And so, more out of curiosity than anything else, the person asks you, "What exactly is the church?"

How would you respond? What would be your definition of church? I'm guessing that a lot of us might begin by explaining that the church is where those who hold a common conviction about Jesus Christ as their risen Savior come together. Typically that happens in a sanctuary on Sunday morning, but it's by no means limited to a steepled building with stained glass. Jesus said it could occur wherever two or more are gathered in his name (Matthew 18:20). Consequently, the church is not so much a particular place as it is a particular people who share the same faith and follow the same Lord and profess the same beliefs.

That would be a short and sweet definition for the church. But of course, like most short, sweet definitions, it doesn't really tell the whole story. Christians share *some* beliefs, to be sure. However, we are a long way from embracing *every* belief. In the United States alone, for example, there are over 900 Protestant denominations. There are Baptists, Methodists, and Episcopalians. There are Presbyterians, Lutherans, and Congregationalists. There are Seventh-day Adventists and Assembly of God, Moravians, and

Quakers. And that's only for starters. It seems as if new denominations spring up, even as the old ones split up. Thus, the question is no longer: "Are you a Baptist?" but "What kind of Baptist?"

When Jesus took a loaf of bread and announced, "This is my body broken for you" (1 Corinthians 11:24), it's difficult to imagine that, even in his most cynical of moments, he would have ever envisioned the church we have today. But part of the reason for this diversity is that we all tend to have our different opinions. One group reads the Bible more literally than another. Some ordain women as ministers and some don't. The emphasis over here might be on salvation, while over there it's on social justice. Let's face it: it's not our beliefs that keep the church together. Most of the time just the opposite is true. Our beliefs are what tear us apart.

So, getting back to this imaginary friend who is inquiring about the church, what should we tell him/her? After all, if it's not our convictions that unite us as Christians, what is it? Some have suggested that it's our common work. In other words, despite our varied understandings of scripture and theology, every denomination still engages in some sort of mission. As a matter of fact, there are even occasions when we seem able to set our differences aside in order to feed the hungry, shelter the homeless, care for the sick, and lift up the downtrodden and oppressed.

Perhaps then, it's not so much our shared beliefs that make us the "one holy, catholic church" — as the Apostles' Creed puts it — but our shared commitment to doing the work of Jesus Christ. The only difficulty I have with this definition is that, rather than saying too little, it almost says too much. Whether we like to admit it or not, the church has never had a patent on kindness, charity, and good will toward others. There are a lot of organizations which feed the hungry and shelter the homeless. They may not be doing it in the name of Jesus Christ (as we are), but they're doing it all the same.

Which, of course, returns us to the original question: only, by this time, it may not be just our hypothetical friend who is confused. Some of you may be wondering: What exactly *is* the church? Surely there must be something that holds us all together and makes us distinct — whether we are Pentecostals or Presbyterians. Still, if it's not our common beliefs or our common work, what on earth would it be?

Well, according to the Apostle Paul, it's none other than Christ himself. "Now you are the body of Christ," he writes to the Corinthians, "and individually members of it" (v. 27). The eye cannot say to the hand, "I have no need of you." Nor should the head suggest to the feet, "Since we do different things, you should belong to a different body." It's all connected. Each part is indispensable to the whole, says Paul. The implication being that, in the church, rather than splitting into groups that think and act in a similar fashion, a better approach might actually be to seek out folks who have a different perspective and maybe even a different agenda. After all, you don't have a body — or at least not a healthy one — unless you have diversity.

It's a powerful image that rings true primarily because we recognize that, within our own physical bodies, there is an amazing diversity. Indeed, we depend upon it. Our liver is meant to function differently than our lungs, and none of us would want either of them suddenly swapping jobs. If our colon were trying to behave like our collarbone, or our ears like our elbows, we would be in a good deal of trouble (not to mention a great amount of pain). We even have parts that most of us don't know the names of, but, thankfully, they don't ever go on strike for being under-appreciated. They just keep on doing whatever it is they do to keep us alive. The bottom line is that we count on our individual parts operating independently, while at the same time working together. And we are quite content to live with such diversity, if for no other reason than we wouldn't live long without it!

It's when you take this analogy and apply it to the church that we start having problems. Apparently, we are able to handle internal variety much better than external variety. Frankly, a lot of us become a little uncomfortable when we run into people who look at the world differently than we do and express viewpoints that challenge our deeply cherished beliefs or disturb our well established routines. As Barbara Brown Taylor once put it, most conflicts in the church develop because "the brains want everybody to act like brains and the hearts wants everybody to act like hearts and there is always a hangnail who brings out the hangnail in everyone else."[1]

Paul's analogy of the church as a body may look great on paper. However, it begins to break down when you actually put it into practice. For example, he says that "if one member suffers, all suffer together with it; if one member is honored, all rejoice together with it" (v. 26). But let's be honest — while I may feel sorry when you are hurting, if someone hits you in the arm, my skin is not going to bruise. Likewise, when you get a pay raise, my standard of living does not go up. The truth of the matter is that when one member of the church suffers, the vast majority don't even know about it, much less feel it. If somebody is honored, the rest of us may applaud, but we rarely experience the same joy that we would if we were receiving the recognition ourselves.

So, if it doesn't square with reality, why is Paul using this particular analogy? One possible reason is that the Corinthians were already familiar with it. Many of the famous Greek and Roman orators employed this same image to explain the nature of the state. In effect, they tried to persuade individual citizens that, just like the various parts of their bodies, the health and efficiency of the country required everyone staying on task and performing their different jobs. Hence, the idea of unity through diversity — that is, functioning independently in order to work together — would not have been seen by the Corinthians as a contradiction in terms. They were well aware that their very survival as a nation depended not so much upon their commonality, but upon their variety.

Paul simply takes this analogy and extends it from the country to the church — only with one significant alteration. He no longer uses it as an analogy. Notice that Paul does not say, "You are *like* the body of Christ." He says, "You *are* the body of Christ." In other words, for Paul the question is not: "Do you want to be Christ's body?" That question has been rendered irrelevant, because whether we want to or not, we already are his body here on earth. A more appropriate question would be: "Are we ready to start acting like Christ's body?"

For instance, every once in a while, someone will tell me of a family who is worshiping elsewhere. "We lost another one to the

Methodists," they'll say. But that's like the heart saying, "I keep losing blood to the legs," or the stomach saying, "I keep losing valuable nutrients to the muscles." If someone is serving Christ in a different congregation — or for that matter, a different denomination — we haven't lost them. We only lose them if, instead of going to church, they decide to sit at home on Sunday morning and read the newspaper.

The point is that we are all part of the same body. It makes no difference whether we realize it or not, whether we agree with it or not, whether we desire it or not. If Paul is correct, it's not something open for debate, which is why we are wasting our time whenever we get involved in these lengthy arguments of who should be in or out of the church. It's Christ's body; he decides. Period. Exclamation point. End of discussion.

Maybe the reason this analogy tends to break down is because it was never meant to be an analogy in the first place. Paul is not trying to describe the church. He wants to define it. Only his definition is not based on a particular philosophy or practice. It's based on the person of Jesus Christ. After all, it was never the disciples' idea to establish the church. They didn't come together the way like-minded people who share similar interests come together to form a club. Nor did they come together the way people with a common passion come together to lobby for a particular cause. They came together because Jesus called them to come together.

And the same is true of us. It's Christ who chose us, Christ who connects us, Christ who consecrates us. He's the one who makes us the holy, catholic church. So the next time someone asks you, "What exactly is the church?" You can tell them, "We are the body of Christ, and individually members of it."

---

1. Barbara Brown Taylor, *Bread of Angels* (Boston: Cowley Publications, 1997), p. 87.

**Epiphany 4
Ordinary Time 4
1 Corinthians 13:1-13**

Losing That Loving Feeling

The thirteenth chapter of First Corinthians is not only the most memorable passage that the Apostle Paul ever wrote; it is arguably the most familiar passage in all of scripture. Even those who are not especially religious, and whose entire experience of church is that they happened to get married in one, have probably come across these words before. "If I speak in the tongues of mortals and of angels ... when I was a child, I spoke like a child ... for now we see in a mirror, dimly, but then we shall see face to face ... so faith, hope, and love abide, these three; and the greatest of these is love." For many of us these verses have become like old, trusted friends. No matter how long it's been since we last visited, they express truths so timeless and profound that just sharing their company has a way of instructing and inspiring us.

In a sense, this chapter represents Paul's attempt to describe the governing rule for Christian life. In Jesus' day, as you may recall, the Jewish faith had become a religion saturated with regulations and ceremonial requirements. There were so many, in fact, that they were almost impossible to keep track of, let alone fulfill. The only folks who even came close were the Pharisees and scribes, and that was only because they were the ones chiefly responsible for this ridiculously complex system in the first place. They spent hours carefully dissecting the Mosaic code — adding amendments, quibbling over exemptions, tinkering with the fine print — until whatever life was still stirring within the law had all but suffocated in the dense smoke of legalese.

Jesus, on the other hand, saw the law quite differently. It wasn't that he wanted to throw all of the rules out the window. He simply wanted to open a window so that the spirit of the law could breathe again. According to Jesus, the supreme requirement is that we love God with all our hearts, souls, minds, and our neighbors as ourselves. "On these two commandments hang all the law and the prophets" is how he put it to the Pharisees (Matthew 22:40). A little later, when he was alone with his disciples, he narrows the focus even further by telling them, "This is my commandment, that you love one another as I have loved you" (John 15:12). The implication being that the only law they really need to keep track of is the Law of Love. If they obey that, they will already be on track in terms of keeping the rest of it.

Love is the one thing, above all else, which our Lord requires of us as disciples, and thus it is the primary characteristic of our faith. If someone were to inquire, "What does it mean to be a Christian?" I don't think you can find a better answer than to say, "It means that we love one another." And if by chance there would be the follow-up question, "What does it mean to love one another?" you can find no better example than the life of Jesus Christ. He did more than merely tell us to love our neighbors; he also taught us how. His intent, it seems, was to move us to the point where we finally love everybody we meet — including those we just met and even those we wish we never had.

But while Jesus clearly demonstrated love for us, he never actually defines it in so many words. This may be the reason we have come to value the significance of 1 Corinthians 13, because what Paul is striving to do here is to spell out exactly what love entails. It's almost as if Jesus presented the heavenly dimensions of love and Paul provides us with the down-to-earth details. "Love is patient; love is kind; love is not envious or boastful or arrogant or rude. It does not insist on its own way; it is not irritable or resentful; it does not rejoice in wrongdoing, but rejoices in the truth. It bears all things, believes all things, hopes all things, endures all things" (vv. 4-7).

Without a doubt, this is one of the most eloquent recitals on the qualities of love ever composed. But curiously, Paul leaves out the one adjective I so frequently hear attributed to love, and that is the adjective "confusing." We might as well admit that for a lot of us this many-splendored thing called love is awfully hard to figure out. It may "make the world go 'round," but in the process it's liable to make your head spin too. For starters, we use the word in a myriad of different ways. A single conversation can produce statements as varied as "I love tennis," and in the next breath, "I love my husband," and a little later, "I love strolling on the beach at sunset." We'll speak of loving everything from movies to milkshakes to Mary Tyler Moore, despite the fact that we obviously don't love all of those in the same manner or even to the same degree.

If that weren't confusing enough, we employ the word to explain about any behavior that you could possibly imagine, no matter how imprudent. "I did it out of love" has practically become a one-size-fits-all rationalization. A man gets involved in an adulterous affair and seems persuaded that this is love. The preacher begs to differ and calls it sin. The wife of an alcoholic picks up the pieces after her husband's latest drinking binge. She claims she is doing it because of love, but the psychologist deems it enabling. A parent indulges all of his/her child's wishes, thinking that is love. The family therapist thinks otherwise and labels it codependency. No wonder we're confused. It's not just that the word is commonly misunderstood, it's that it is so casually misappropriated. I guess you could say that the word *love* is linguistically-challenged.

However, from what I've observed, the problem actually goes much deeper than that. As I counsel with people regarding their relationships, what I find is that far too many of us view love as a feeling rather than a choice. That is, we see love strictly as an emotion instead of an act. To some extent, this confusion is entirely natural — indeed, it's almost to be expected — because it stems from our earliest encounters with love as adolescents. That is when most of us initially stumbled into this magical, dreamlike, rose-colored, and hormone-driven world called love.

Don't you remember the first time you fell in love? There you were, hovering above the ground as your feet bounced from cloud to cloud. Suddenly the whole world seemed different to you — flowers bloomed, birds sang, stars twinkled. During class you would doodle the other person's name on your notebook, and whenever you saw him/her, your heart skipped a beat. Both of you would ride home together on the school bus holding hands, and then rush to call each other on the telephone — because, my goodness, it had been a whole five minutes since you last spoke! All of the symptoms were there and they all pointed to the same diagnosis. You were hopelessly, head-over-heels in lo-o-ove.

Fortunately, most of us eventually discover that that's not really love; it's infatuation. However, the feelings which accompany it are so intense — and let's face it, so euphoric — that we can't help but desire to experience those feelings again. As a matter of fact, a lot of us go out looking to experience them again. I'm not sure if there's a twelve-step program for this sort of thing, but perhaps there ought to be, because the sheer excitement of being "in love" is addictive. That's why, even when we move beyond adolescent infatuation and enter into a more mature relationship, we still expect that it will give us the warm, wonderful sensation of walking on the clouds with our heart all aflutter. In short, the emotions that were involved the first time we fell in love begin to define every other time.

I frequently run into this during premarital counseling, as I try to persuade couples that their wedding is not an opportunity to demonstrate how madly in love they both are. What I point out is that neither bride nor groom are ever asked if they happen to *feel* lovingly toward one another. Everybody already assumes that — and besides, usually it's so obvious that even the flower girl and ring bearer are blushing. The reason we have gathered is to witness their promises to *act* lovingly "in plenty and in want, in joy and in sorrow, in sickness and in health, as long as we both shall live."

But despite my efforts to convince them otherwise, most couples still seem to think that, hidden somewhere in those vows, is an unspoken assurance that their marriage will always have that certain blissful feeling. And for a while it does! It's what we call "the honeymoon." However, as I'm sure many of you will attest, that doesn't last. It never lasts. Indeed, it *cannot* last, precisely because it's a feeling — and feelings, by definition, come and go.

Perhaps an illustration will prove helpful. Let me briefly describe what a feeling is. It's the fourth component of an emotional response. For example, consider the feeling of fear. Imagine that you are out on a hike this afternoon. You're strolling down a wooded path, and suddenly in front of you — just a few feet away, coiled and ready to strike — is a copperhead snake. Needless to say, for most of us this is going to elicit an emotional response (and judging from the panicked look on some of your faces, it already has). That response is made up of five components.

The first part is an involuntary action. You stop. You don't say to yourself, "I think now would be a good time to stop." It happens automatically.

Then comes the second part. Within your body, all kinds of internal changes begin to take place — your heartbeat increases, the blood starts pumping, your adrenaline kicks in, and so forth.

Next is part three. You react. You run, you jump, you scream — whatever is your custom when you meet up with a copperhead snake.

The fourth part is a feeling. All of these internal changes produce a feeling. In this case, it's likely to be the feeling of fear.

And then, once you're safely out of danger, comes the fifth part, as your body adjusts back to normal.

But here's the thing — all of this, from start to finish, is involuntary. It's not something that any of us choose to do or even contemplate in advance. Our bodies are already predisposed to react in this manner, and part of that automatic, involuntary reaction is that we *feel* something. This is why, with regard to adolescent infatuation, we often characterize it as "falling in love." It isn't a conscious decision. No one plans to fall in love. Most of the time we're not even prepared for it. We're just making our way through life, minding our own business, and in glides old Cupid with his quiver of amorous arrows, and — zing! — that's it, we're smitten.

Incidentally, the Greeks had a word for this. They called it *eros*, and it was actually one of three words that they had for love (the other two being the sympathetic *philia* shared among friends and the merciful *agape* of God). *Eros*, though, was the most common, and it was used to describe any relationship which develops as a result of our needs and desires. It's what we keep hoping will satisfy our cravings, and assuage our appetites, and, ultimately, fill the emptiness we all seem to carry around within us. It's that love which is forever crying out, "I want! I need!"

Not so with *agape* (the kind of love Paul is speaking of here). *Agape* does not want. It gives. *Agape* does not need. It serves. *Agape* is not an emptiness desperately trying to be filled. It is already overflowing. Indeed, part of Paul's intent throughout this chapter is to get us to recognize the distinction between *eros* and *agape*. *Agape* is patient, he says. *Eros* is restless and moody. *Agape* is accepting and willing to endure all things. *Eros* stubbornly clings to its own agenda and accepts nothing less. *Agape* never ends, while *eros* — even in its noblest forms — ceases the moment the object of our attraction becomes unattractive. In a word, *eros* is something we feel and *agape* is something we choose.

For the Christian, therefore, love is not primarily a feeling. It doesn't happen automatically, because it's not an involuntary response. It's something we have control over. That is, we can choose to love. When Jesus said, "Love your enemies," he wasn't implying that we should have warm, fuzzy feelings about them. If that were the case, he would be asking us to do something that we simply don't have the power to do. You can't manufacture a warm, fuzzy feeling anymore than you can manufacture a sneeze or a yawn. What he's saying is: "Choose to love them. Decide to love them."

Some of us might object, "But, Jesus, I don't even like them that much." To which Jesus would respond, "So what? I'm not asking you to like them; I'm asking you to love them."

"But, Jesus, I don't know if I can feel that way about them."

"I'm not asking you to *feel* something," says Jesus, "I'm asking you to *do* something."

"But, Jesus, don't you have to feel it first? Doesn't it have to come from the heart to be authentic? I don't what to be phony about it."

"I can appreciate that," says Jesus. "But if you're the one who decides to do it — sincerely, earnestly, willingly, honestly — how can it be phony? It's not something you just felt like doing. It's something you chose to do."

Of course, there's a catch to all of this. You knew there would be one, right? Here's the catch. If you decide to love someone — putting their interests ahead of yours and working for their happiness and well-being, even if it means sacrificing your own — you may find that, in the end, you start feeling something for them too. The Apostle Paul says that, of all the gifts God has given us, love is the greatest. It is the most powerful force that exists. But to some extent, it is also the most powerless, because it can do nothing except by our consent. We need to decide to love. It's not a feeling; it's a choice.

**Epiphany 5
Ordinary Time 5
1 Corinthians 15:1-11**

Sharing What We Have Been Shown

This passage is not exactly gossip, although it comes pretty close. Even Paul seems to admit as much. "For I handed on to you as of first importance," he writes, "what I in turn had received" (v. 3). In other words, he is not offering us an eyewitness account here; he's simply reporting what he has been told, which is understandable when you consider that Paul wasn't in Jerusalem on that fateful Easter weekend. He didn't see the crucifixion. He played no part in the funeral procession. He never even visited the empty tomb.

Paul didn't experience any of this firsthand. But he obviously knew people who had, and presumably it's from them that he has gathered his information. The way he heard it, during those forty days following the resurrection, the risen Christ appeared first to Cephas, then to the other disciples, and not long after that, to over 500 believers at the same time. "If you don't believe me," he tells the Corinthians, "you can ask them for yourselves, since most of them are still around and would be happy to describe what it was like." Our Lord came next to James, and then to the rest of the apostles, and last of all — maybe even least of all, adds Paul — he found me.

You can't help wishing, of course, that we knew a little more about each of these appearances. There is just enough here to tantalize. For example, did that initial revelation to Peter take place as he was returning from the tomb? Luke seems to indicate that, while the others scoffed at the story, Peter actually went down there to check it out (Luke 24:12). Maybe that's when Christ met him. Or what about this assembly of 500 — when did that occur? None of the Gospels mention such an event, unless it's implied in that vague reference to the risen Lord performing "many convincing proofs" (Acts 1:3). And which James is this exactly? Was it John's brother, the son of Zebedee? Or the so-called "James the younger," the son of Alphaeus? Some have suggested that it was none other than Jesus' brother. However, since he was not a follower during Jesus' lifetime, it would be interesting to learn when and how he became one.

Paul doesn't provide us with many details. He simply recites the litany of appearances as if it was all a well-established fact. But if this same testimony were presented in a court of law, it would almost certainly be dismissed as hearsay, because apart from his own personal encounter, Paul offers no evidence whatsoever. Indeed, the great irony of this passage is that the lack of proof was probably one of the strongest arguments that Saul the Pharisee used against the Christians, back when he was trying to snuff this fledgling movement out of existence.

Bear in mind that there had been suspicions all along that the disciples might be planning an elaborate hoax, and that soon the rumors would be flying that Jesus of Nazareth had risen from the dead. Matthew says the chief priests even approached Pilate with this scenario and suggested that Roman guards be stationed at the tomb just in case. However, since Pilate had hardly been in favor of crucifying Jesus to begin with, he was not about to dispatch military personnel to babysit the man's corpse. "Don't you have a guard of soldiers?" he asked sarcastically. "Go and make it as secure as you can" (Matthew 27:65), which is precisely what they did — or at least what they *attempted* to do. When Jesus shook loose the shackles of death and walked out of the cemetery, the chief priests quickly decided that perhaps a rumor was better than the truth after all. So they concocted the wild tale that, as the guards were taking their rest, the disciples had taken the body (Matthew 28:11-13).

I'm sure that's the explanation Saul preferred, and no doubt the one he most actively promoted. In his mind, the Christians were nothing more than a bunch of grave robbers playing on the superstitions of the gullible and naïve. "This talk of a resurrection is absolute nonsense," he likely told the congregations, as he moved from synagogue to synagogue. "Where is the evidence? What proof do they have?" He might even have pointed out that all of these alleged sightings involved folks who were already believers.

And actually, as far as that goes, Saul would have been correct. Because according to the Gospel accounts, Christ reveals himself only to the faithful. Don't ask me why. If I had been Jesus' campaign manager, I would have run the resurrection a little differently and scheduled some public appearances. I think the thing to have done would be to have the risen Christ parade up and down the main streets of Jerusalem or stand out in front of the Temple so that the crowds could ooh and aah in amazement. Better still, I would have had him march straight into Pilate's headquarters and announce, "Well, Pontius, do you want to give it another shot?"

But that's not what our Lord does. He never visits Pilate or Caiaphas or any of the chief priests. He comes only to those who had been willing to come to him in the first place. Of course, the one notable exception is that he met Saul on the road to Damascus. However, even then, it's not the physical evidence that finally persuades Saul; it's the experience. It's almost as if Christ is not interested in proving the resurrection as an intellectual proposition. What he desires is a relationship, not just a realization.

The bottom line is that our risen Lord manifests himself exclusively to the church. We're the ones who witnessed his life, death, and resurrection, and therefore, we are the ones responsible for declaring it to the world. If people don't know what took place on Easter, it's not Pilate's fault. We can't blame the government for not getting the message out. Christ came to us. This is our story to tell.

I think that's why Paul wants to go over it again with the Corinthians. "Now I would remind you, brothers and sisters, of the good news that I proclaimed to you, which you in turn received, in which also you stand, [and] through which also you are being saved" (vv. 1-2). In effect, Paul is encouraging the Corinthians to claim their identity as children of the resurrection. The reason he's reminding them of these things is because this is precisely the good news that they now need to share. And the same is true for us.

Occasionally someone will lament to me that our culture no longer seems to be very Christian-friendly. For example, it used to be that on Sunday mornings pretty much everything else was closed except for the church. Shopping at the mall or going to an amusement park was simply not an option. But, of course, that's no longer the case. Most schools have started referring to "Christmas Vacation" as "Winter Break." Federal courts have taken up the debate of whether the Pledge of Allegiance can be recited in the classroom because of the phrase "one nation under God." Some of you may even have noticed that there are now soccer games routinely scheduled for Sunday mornings — including Easter!

Like many of you, I lament this as well. However, I am not inclined to dash an angry letter off to the school board or the soccer association. And I'll tell you why. It's not their responsibility to promote Christianity; it's ours. I've gone through the Gospels, time and time again, and I cannot find a single instance where our risen Lord ever appeared to the soccer association. He did not visit the school board or the city council. He never held a public hearing in the town square.

We can whine and complain all we want, but that's not going to change the fact that we cannot expect the general population to carry forth the Christian message, unless we share it with them. If the true meaning of Easter is lost and dwindles down to little more than colored eggs and bunny rabbits, it's not the school's fault or the government's fault or the society's fault. If that happens, it will be the church's fault, because the risen Christ came to us. And if the world is going to believe that he got up from the grave, it will only be because we, who believe it, start declaring it.

Let me see if I can get you to picture this. Suppose you have friends who have recently purchased a new boat, and they are excitedly telling you about it. They describe how big it is, and how powerful, and how luxurious. "It sounds great," you finally say. "When are you taking it out on the water?"

"Oh, we're not going to take this boat out on the water," they reply.

"You're not?"

"No way; it might get damaged. There are all kinds of things that could happen to it out there. It could get scratched; it could get stuck. Our boat is staying on the land."

"Are you trying to tell me that you just bought a boat that you're never going to use?"

"But we are going to use it," your friends inform you. "That's the best part. You see, we belong to a club where we all keep our boats in this huge garage. We never take them out on the water. We go down there once a week and we polish our boats and sit up on the deck and wave at one another."

"You're kidding me, right?"

"No, we're serious. It's a lot of fun. We tell boat stories, and sing boat songs, and learn all of the rules for safe boating."

"But none of you are ever going to take your boats out?"

"Probably not," your friends say. "Every once in a while, we'll invite somebody who has actually been out on the water to come in and tell us what it's like. They'll talk for a little bit and answer our questions. Sometimes they'll even bring slides, so that we can see how it would be if we ever went out on the water ourselves. And usually we'll take up a little offering for them."

Do you see what I'm getting at? I hope that we are not just coming here once a week to tell boat stories, and sing boat songs, and learn about boats from others who actually go out on the water. The reason the risen Christ has come to us is so that we will go out into the world. After all, everyone already knows that Jesus lived. That's a matter of public record. Everyone already knows that Jesus died. That, too, is a matter of public record. But when it comes to the resurrection of Jesus Christ, that's not a matter of public record. Of that, *we* are the witnesses.

Epiphany 6
Ordinary Time 6
1 Corinthians 15:12-20

The Son Also Rises

When it comes to the resurrection, one of the things that all of the Gospel writers agree upon is that nobody was expecting it. Even the disciples seem to have been caught by surprise. This is actually kind of surprising in and of itself, considering that on at least three different occasions Jesus took the disciples aside and told them exactly what to expect. "See, we are going up to Jerusalem," he explained, "and the Son of Man will be handed over to the chief priests and the scribes, and they will condemn him to death; then they will hand him over to the Gentiles; they will mock him, and spit upon him, and flog him, and kill him; and after three days he will rise again" (Mark 10:33-34).

Now I'm not sure how he could have put it any more plainly than that. He practically gives the disciples an hour-by-hour itinerary. But apparently, they never took Jesus at his word. They literally didn't think that he would live up to it. That's why there is no receiving line at the tomb. No one shows up on Easter with a "Welcome Back" banner and a fresh change of clothes for the Master. Indeed, one gets the impression that the disciples had no intention of showing up at all.

They send the women to the cemetery instead. And as far as I can tell, they aren't any more eager to make this trip than were the men. The only reason they trudge down there at the crack of dawn is to anoint the body with spices. Ordinarily, they would have attended to that ceremonial matter prior to his burial. But in this case, since Jesus' body was removed from the cross just hours before sunset and the beginning of the Sabbath, they ran out of time.

So, first thing Sunday morning, before the sun even came up, they set out on their lonely pilgrimage. Why so early? It could be that this was their way of coping with Jesus' death. Sometimes, when your grief is too heavy and the pain too fresh, you just try to stay busy. You concentrate on the things that need to be done, and occupy your thoughts with various chores here and there, so that you can keep on keeping on. However, I'm guessing that the main reason for their pre-dawn departure is to avoid the snickering crowds, with all of their snide comments: "What happened to your Wonder Boy? Some Messiah he turned out to be!" These women aren't really in the mood for that right now. They just want to go to the tomb and get it over with — the sooner the better.

The last thing they expected is that the tomb would be empty. I've always thought that question the angel poses in Luke's Gospel, "Why do you seek the living among the dead?" (Luke 24:5), missed the point. They weren't seeking the *living* among the dead; they were seeking the *dead* among the dead. They were not looking to find anything in that cemetery but a corpse. And maybe a few guards, who somehow got stuck with the most impossible assignment in military history, that of trying to keep the Lord of Life in the grave.

The bottom line is that the resurrection was not anticipated by anybody. Even the Apostle Paul had trouble believing that Christ had risen from the dead, until he was practically knocked half-dead himself on the road to Damascus. It was an experience that left him blind for three days. But in a sense, it also opened his eyes. Never again would he be able to look at life — or even death — the same way. More than anything else, that seems to be the source of his concern with the Corinthians. Paul couldn't understand why on earth they would want to go back to their old worldview. "Now if Christ is proclaimed as raised from the dead, how can some of you say there is no resurrection from the dead?" (v. 12).

It's hard to read these words without having the sense that he is speaking here not just theologically, but very personally as well. For Paul, the resurrection is the linchpin of the Christian faith. Remove it and everything else falls away — including us! If the real flesh-and-blood Jesus Christ, who was crucified dead as dead can be, did not get up on that first Sunday, then there's not much sense in our getting up and going to church any Sunday thereafter. "Everything I have been preaching to you has been a lie," says Paul. "What's more, everything you've been doing has been a complete waste of time." Granted, he had told them earlier that "we are all fools for Christ's sake." But there's a difference between appearing foolish and actually *being* foolish. Playing the fool will at least get you some laughs now and then. However, the way Paul sees it, if the resurrection never happened, then we shouldn't be laughed at; we should be pitied (v. 19b).

Hence, what he strives to do in this passage is to provide the Corinthians with a rationale for believing in the resurrection. The argument he offers is a deductive one. That is, it moves along a logical chain of reasoning, one link at a time.

> *If there is no resurrection of the dead ...*
> *... then Christ has not been raised*
> *And if Christ has not been raised ...*
> *... then our preaching was a lie ...*
> *And if our preaching was a lie ...*
> *... then your faith is futile.*

It sounds solid. But as anyone who has ever studied logic will tell you, in order for this kind of argument to work, it has to be anchored somewhere. In other words, I need to offer some evidence of the initial proposition. If you accept the first link in the logical chain as an established fact, then the rest will follow. If you don't, the whole thing immediately falls apart.

I am indebted to Thomas Long for this insight. He suggests that we think of it this way. Suppose I am trying to convince you that a mutual friend, Ernie, was absent from church last Sunday. It obviously won't do much good for me just to insist repeatedly that he was not there. If you are skeptical that I'm telling the truth, I need an argument. So I construct the following: "If Ernie was in San Antonio last Sunday, then he could not have been here in our town, and if he wasn't here, he, therefore, could not have been present in our church." So far, so good; the logical chain makes sense. But it only works to the extent that I can prove the first link in that chain of reasoning. Thus, I need a photograph of him standing in front of the Alamo, or a receipt from a restaurant on the River Walk, or something of the sort that will verify for you, and anyone else who is interested, that Ernie was, indeed, in San Antonio last Sunday. If I can produce the evidence at the beginning, then the rest can be logically deduced.

However, as Long points out, in these kinds of arguments, sometimes the proof is not at the beginning, but at the end. So, to return to our example, I say to you, "If Ernie was in San Antonio last Sunday, then he was not in our town, and if we wasn't here, he couldn't have been in church." At which point, you respond, "But he was in our church last Sunday. He sang in the choir. He was part of my Sunday school class. I shook hands with him as we were Passing the Peace." In other words, because you know and trust your own experience, the logic of the argument now runs the other way. Ernie was definitely in our church; therefore he could not have been in San Antonio as you claim.

I think that's precisely how this argument from Paul is meant to work. It taps into our own experience. "If there is no resurrection of the dead," says Paul, "then Christ has not been raised. And if Christ has not been raised, then our preaching was a lie. And if our preaching was a lie, then your faith is futile." At which point, the Corinthians would have surely responded, "But our faith is not futile!" Even the Corinthians — as badly divided as they were — knew that their faith meant something, because they had experienced the risen Christ.[1]

The same is true for you and me, of course. We do not need to conduct a congregational expedition back to the empty tomb, and weigh out all of the evidence to discern whether it is true. Go to the places in your life where you know it's true, because you have already encountered the risen Christ.

Go back to that dark valley, where you could barely see because of the tears in your eyes, and you didn't know how you were going to make it through the end of the day ... and then you felt a gentle hand upon your shoulder and a voice whispering in your ear: "Do not be afraid, I'm here with you."

Go back to that time when you tossed and turned all night, anguishing over a decision for which there were no easy answers and every alternative carried a certain degree of risk. You didn't know for the life of you which way to turn ... and somewhere, somehow, you felt a strength not your own, which said: "Trust me, I will look after you."

Go back to that occasion when you were struggling to believe in yourself, and your entire life seemed pointless ... and suddenly you felt the embrace of Christ's love, providing you with the assurance that you count for something in this world, and in the next.

I guess what I'm trying to say is that we don't need to explain the resurrection. The resurrection explains us. We know our faith is not futile. And if our faith is not futile, then our preaching has not been a lie. And if our preaching has not been a lie, then Christ has been raised from the dead. And if Christ has been raised from the dead, then so shall we.

---

1. Thomas Long, "The Easter Sermon," *Journal for Preachers*, Vol. X, No. 3, pp. 6-7.

**Epiphany 7
Ordinary Time 7
1 Corinthians 15:35-38, 42-50**

Revised And Amended
By The Author Of Life

The celebrated theologian and novelist Frederick Buechner once remarked that preaching is like doing algebra. An intriguing comparison, to be sure. But to use his example, consider the equation $x + y = z$. If you know the value of one of these letters, then you know at least something. If you know the value of two, you can probably figure the rest of it out and solve the whole thing. If you aren't sure of the value of any, then you are pretty much stuck.

Preachers would do well to remember this, especially when they start flinging phrases from the pulpit like "the blood atonement of Jesus Christ," or "the communion of saints," or even "the resurrection of the body." Such abstract doctrines are likely to remain just that — abstract — unless one knows the particular value and meaning of each word. As Buechner observes:

> *If preachers make no attempt to flesh out these words in terms of everyday human experience (maybe even their own) but simply repeat with variations the same old formulas week after week, then the congregation might just as well spend Sunday morning at home with the funnies ... If people's understanding of theological phrases goes little deeper than their dictionary or catechetical definitions, then to believe in them has just about as much effect on their lives as to believe that Columbus discovered America in 1492 or that $x + y = z$.*[1]

Simply put, it is never wise to have a sermon filled with too many variables.

This brings us to the morning's scripture lesson. Since Paul is speaking in this passage about things that no one really knows about with any degree of certainty, we probably shouldn't hold him to mathematical exactness. He does his best, of course, to express the inexpressible and describe the indescribable. However, I think even he would admit that, in terms of understanding the great and glorious mysteries of heaven, we will never succeed in solving all of the variables.

Having said that, the question that Paul is attempting to answer for the Corinthians is: "What kind of body will we have in the life to come?" Because he can't help but do otherwise, Paul responds to this question with a series of analogies. To begin with, he compares it to a seed. "What you sow does not come to life unless it dies," he points out. "And as for what you sow, you do not sow the body that is to be, but a bare seed, perhaps of wheat or some other grain. But God gives it a body as he has chosen, and to each kind of seed its own body" (vv. 36-38). In other words, when you put a seed in the ground, it dies. In due time and under the right conditions, it will rise again. Only it will do so with a radically different body than that with which it was sown.

Still, it's not as if the plant has an entirely separate existence from the seed. Distinct, yes; different, to be sure; but not separate. One life leads to the other. In effect, what Paul is trying to demonstrate here is that, at one and the same time, there can be dissolution, difference, and yet continuity. The seed dissolves in order to bring forth a different life, but it remains an extension of the same seed. Likewise, our earthly bodies will dissolve and rise again in a very different form. However, it is the same person who rises. Dissolved by death and transformed by resurrection, it is still we who exist.

This is not to suggest, of course, that we are immortal. Being immortal implies that we are death-proof — or at least, our souls are. To believe in the immortality of the soul is to believe that while our bodies may lie moldering in the dirt, our souls go marching bravely on because — well, because that's just what souls do. They don't die, because they can't die. True or false as that may be, it's not what the Bible teaches. The scriptural view is that our body and soul are as inextricably bound to one another as seed and plant.

Put another way, we don't just *have* some body, we *are* somebody. Thus, when we kick the bucket, we kick it a hundred percent — body and soul. There is no part of us that automatically lives on. If that were the case, there would be no need for a resurrection at all. What Christians believe is that when we die, that's it — we're dead! Then, by God's mighty power and merciful grace, we are given our lives back again, just as we were given those lives by God the first time around.

According to Paul, though, while our heavenly life will certainly be different than the one we currently enjoy, it won't be some disembodied remnant, or distant echo, of what we are here on earth. On the contrary, the same unique qualities and characteristics that make us *some* body, and not just *any* body, will remain intact. This is precisely what we are affirming when we speak of "the resurrection of the body." We're not referring to our physical bodies (frankly, I'm looking forward to trading this one in some day for a sleeker model). What we mean is that our personality — or better yet, our personhood — continues on.

When a child dies, for instance, we ought not to think of him/her as forever remaining a child in heaven. It's the personhood — the individuality, if you like — that is resurrected. It's all of those wonderful gifts and abilities that were already present in the child, only we never had a chance to see them fully developed. But one day we will, because one day we shall all be reunited in a kingdom whose love knows no bounds, and whose life has no end. Does this imply that we will be able to recognize one another in heaven? I believe so, absolutely. We won't look the same, of course. But then again, we won't see the same either. We will be given the ability to recognize in each other the very things that prejudice, hatred, and jealousy so often prevent us from seeing now.

That seems to be what Paul is getting at in his second analogy. "Not all flesh is alike," he writes, "but there is one flesh for human beings, another for animals, another for birds, and another for fish. There are both heavenly bodies and earthly bodies, but the glory of the heavenly is one thing, and that of the earthly is another" (1 Corinthians 15:39-40). In other words, when God fashioned the heavens and the earth, and flung the stars into the farthest reaches of the galaxies like rice at a wedding, God gave each living thing a body suitable for its specific part and function in creation. For example, did you realize that in order to nurse their young, whales possess a special mechanism that enables their babies to suckle underwater without drowning? Or that to pump blood up to the head of a giraffe requires such a high blood pressure that they would black out each time they bent down for a drink, if it weren't for the fact that they possess a special blood pressure-reducing mechanism, a network of tiny veins called the *rete mirabile*? You see, God has given every creature great and small exactly what they need to live.

In a similar fashion, Paul submits that when we are raised in glory, we will be given a body suitable for the resurrected life. Whether this will entail another kind of anatomy, or simply an improved one — with special eyes, better hearing, upgraded hearts, and the like — is anyone's guess. Paul doesn't speculate on the particulars. The bottom line is that we will all be revised and amended as the Author of our stories sees fit. This much seems certain, however. In the life to come, we will be able to listen to God more closely, know God more deeply, love God more fully, and serve God most faithfully.

Indeed, the reason we will be able to do so is because our bodies will no longer be encumbered by the faults and frailties that we experience here on earth. No longer will we have to deal with the deterioration and decay that our present bodies inevitably incur with the passing of the years. No longer will we be governed by appetites and urges that are never fully satisfied. No longer will we be limited by our physical condition, or judged by our appearance. No longer will the flesh prove willing but the spirit weak, for one will be transformed into the other. The Apostle Paul puts it this way: "What is sown is perishable, what is raised is imperishable. It is sown in dishonor; it is raised in glory. It is sown in weakness; it is raised in power. It is sown a physical body; it is raised a spiritual body" (vv. 42-44).

In effect, what Paul is announcing throughout this passage is that the resurrection completes us. Ultimately we become who we were truly meant to be all along.

But even more significant than that, what I think Paul is saying here is that when the final curtain falls on the drama of life, and all of the actors and actresses are assembled on stage, we will discover that the playwright has penned yet another role for us to perform.

When the present is past and the future is now, God will be there to grant us life again and to lead us forth into a glorious new future.

When the long journey is over and we've reached our intended destination, we will find that our end is also our beginning — together with God.

---

1. Frederick Buechner, *Whistling in the Dark: A Doubter's Dictionary* (San Francisco: HarperCollins Publishers, 1993), pp. 5-6.

**Epiphany 8
Ordinary Time 8
1 Corinthians 15:51-58**

A Labor Not In Vain

According to the book of Acts, when Saul set out toward Damascus with his satchel of arrest warrants, he was a man on a mission. Both would change by the time he got there. Somewhere on that dusty stretch of road north of Jerusalem, he encountered the risen Christ and ended up experiencing a resurrection of his own. It was such a radical conversion that when he later reported it to the Corinthians, he described the entire event in the third person — as if it had actually happened to somebody else. And in a sense, it did. One person died that day and another was born. Saul the Pharisee became Paul the Apostle.

He was never the same afterwards, and of course neither was Christianity. Apart from Jesus, no one had a more profound influence upon the early church than did Paul. He moved back and forth across the Mediterranean world, planting congregations like a farmer scattering seeds. Even imprisonment didn't slow him down. If he had a moment to spare, he would write a letter. He seemed obsessed with keeping in touch with the churches. Only for him it was more a matter of keeping them in touch with Christ. The postage alone must have cost Paul a small fortune. But as it turns out, that was the least of his concerns.

"Five times I have received at the hands of the Jews the forty lashes minus one," he declared. "Three times I was beaten with rods. Once I received a stoning. Three times I was shipwrecked; for a night and a day I was adrift at sea; on frequent journeys, in dangers from rivers ... bandits ... my own people ... Gentiles ... false brothers and sisters" (2 Corinthians 11:24-26).

In other words, Paul didn't just run into trouble, he galloped into it. Everywhere he went there was controversy, and more often than not, he was at the center of it. He argued almost as much with his friends as he did with his enemies. He pushed. He prodded. He pondered. He praised. He preached. Anything to get his point across. However, even among those churches he had helped to establish, the reviews were usually mixed. Paul was revered by some and ridiculed by others.

To be sure, there were times when the pressure of it all got the better of him, and he became so discouraged that he could barely think straight. "I do not understand my own actions," he confessed to the Romans. "For I do not do what I want, but I do the very thing I hate ... I can will what is right, but I cannot do it ... Wretched man that I am! Who will rescue me from this body of death?" Paul probably paused at that point; his hand shaking so badly he was unable to continue. He felt the awful weight of that question. In weaker moments, it was the one thing that had always tormented him. *How can I be saved? Who will deliver me?* And when the answer finally came to Paul, it may well have knocked him to the ground as forcefully as it had back on that dusty road years earlier. "Thanks be to God through Jesus Christ our Lord!" he concluded (Romans 7:15-25).

You can say what you want about Paul, but you have to give him this: He possessed a confidence that even his harshest critics must have secretly admired. He was certain of how salvation worked, and it had nothing to do with how long or hard any of us worked. The way Paul saw it, there was no criterion we had to meet, precisely because there was no criterion we ever could. It was a gift, more or less — which meant that, whatever we did, God wouldn't love us any more or any less.

Paul knew that! Indeed, stating so became one of his favorite expressions. Browse through the epistles sometime and take note of how often he used the phrase "I know." Not "I think." Not "I hope." Not "I have a hunch." Paul never hedged his bet with words like "maybe" or "perhaps." Nor had he been crisscrossing the continent, risking life and limb, just to venture his humble opinion or an educated guess. He was persuaded. He was convinced.

Once when he was in jail awaiting trial, he shared with his friends in Philippi that there was no telling how this would all turn out. To be honest, he wasn't even sure how he wanted it to turn out. As far as he was concerned, whether he lived or died, the end result was basically the same — either way he would be with Christ. "But to remain in the flesh is more necessary for you," he wrote. "Since I am convinced of this, I *know* that I will remain and continue with all of you for your progress and joy in faith" (Philippians 1:24-25, emphasis added).

On another occasion he attended a potluck supper at one of the churches. Everybody brought a dish from home, and as Paul stood in the buffet line he saw that some of the food had been blessed at the local pagan shrine. So he simply had an extra helping of the kosher casserole, lest anyone be offended by what he ate. In reality, though, he recognized that there wasn't anything wrong with the food. "I *know* and am persuaded," he explained, "that nothing in the Lord Jesus is unclean in itself" (Romans 14:14, emphasis added).

Even when confronted with the likelihood of his own execution, and the stench of death loomed so close it stuck in his throat, Paul remained certain of God's grace. *Will anything come between us and Christ's love?* "NO!" he wrote emphatically, bearing down so hard the tip of his pencil snapped. "For I am persuaded that neither death, nor life, nor angels, nor rulers, nor things present, nor things to come, nor powers, nor height, nor depth, nor anything else in all creation will be able to separate us from the love of God in Christ Jesus our Lord" (Romans 8:38-39).

Over and over again, Paul displayed this unshakable confidence. However, for some reason, at the close of this scripture passage, he suddenly decides to switch pronouns. He doesn't say, "I know," he says, "You know." After discussing the promise of the resurrection and of how we shall all be clothed with immortality, Paul encourages the Corinthians to be "steadfast, immovable, always excelling ... because *you know* that in the Lord your labor is not in vain" (v. 58, emphasis added).

That's a rather remarkable claim, when you stop and think about it. After all, how can Paul be so sure that we know our labors are not in vain? Even the writer of Ecclesiastes apparently had his doubts as to whether there was much of a point to any of our busyness. His skeptical take on life was that our frantic pace and hectic schedules accomplished little more than chasing after the wind — which, at times, seems like a fairly apt description.

For example, consider a typical workday. You are jolted awake by the alarm and quickly get the children fed, dressed, and on the school bus. Then you get ready yourself and fight the traffic all the way to the office, where you dance between appointments and deal with a steady barrage of e-mails and conference calls. The same traffic is fought all the way home (only now you're sharing the ride with a stack of assignments that was dropped on your desk at the last minute). You have a hurried dinner with the family, help the kids with their homework, and trot them through the evening routine of bath, books, and bed. You finish up your own work, catch a few stories on the news, and call it a night ... so that tomorrow morning you can be jolted awake and do it all over again!

It's no wonder we occasionally ask ourselves, *Am I really getting anywhere?* Because despite our best efforts to stay on top of everything, it can often feel as if we're climbing stairs of sand. We finally get the car paid off and the transmission goes out. We send the youngest child to college and the oldest one can't find a job and needs to move back home. We take account of our lives and it winds up looking like a handful of loose change. A little is spent here, a little there. But in the greater scheme of things, does what we're doing actually amount to very much?

Paul seems to think so. Moreover, he is convinced that we should be certain of it too. "Keep up the good work and hold firm to the faith," he tells the Corinthians, "because you know that in the Lord your labor is not in vain." And maybe that tiny phrase "in the Lord" is the key to what he's getting at here. Paul is not suggesting that our individual labors will always prove fruitful and productive. He knew better than most that that wasn't the case. As a Pharisee, he had worked harder than anybody, only to find out that he was trying to earn an invitation to a party which didn't even require an RSVP — it was "Come As You Are."

The reason our labors are not in vain is because the risen Christ continues to work through us. It's not a matter of how well we perform; it's how much we will one day be transformed. "Listen, I will tell you a mystery," writes Paul. "We will not all die, but we will all be changed, in a moment, in the twinkling of an eye, at the last trumpet" (vv. 51-52a). Nor is this to be some disembodied life, where we all get mixed together into an ephemeral cloud of cosmic energy. The same qualities and characteristics that made us unique individuals here on earth remain intact. Only now we will be wearing a marvelous new version of corporeality — not of flesh and blood any longer but of spirit — imperishable and immortal.

You see, the way Paul figured it, if death did not mark the end of our Lord's work, then it won't be the end of ours either. Indeed, because we have the promise of another life, we can begin to live this one without all of the encumbrances that tend to weigh us down: things like fear and insecurity, guilt and greed, worry and regret. We now have the freedom to open our arms instead of clinching our fists, to start mending fences instead of slamming doors, to risk something great for something even greater. Simply put, we can be confident that our work here is not in vain, because in Jesus Christ, we know that life has a destination, and not just an end.

Picture it this way. Suppose you were on a cruise, and one afternoon the captain got on the intercom and announced: "Ladies and gentleman, I hope this won't panic anybody. We have plenty of food, plenty of entertainment, and plenty of activities to keep all of you occupied and content. However, we've decided not to head for a port. Instead, we are going to cruise around the ocean until we run out of fuel, and then drift idly along until we sink. Have a pleasant trip."

If you were on such a ship, what would be your reaction? Would you just sit back in your lounge chair and soak up the sunshine? I don't think so. You and I, as well as every other passenger, would be heading for the life rafts and paddling for shore. Not because the cruise wasn't still enjoyable, but because if there is no destination, it's meaningless. And the same is true of life. Enjoyment is not enough. If the only future we can expect is that tomorrow will be a duplicate of today, and the day before that, then our work here really is in vain. In effect, we are merely killing time until time kills us — like an endless game of cards where we're never dealt a new hand.

However, in Jesus Christ, that's precisely what we're given. "For this perishable body must put on imperishability," announces Paul, "and this mortal body must put on immortality. When this perishable body puts on imperishability, and this mortal body puts on immortality, then the saying that is written will be fulfilled: 'Death has been swallowed up in victory' " (vv. 53-54). It is the farthest and deepest his eyes had ever seen into the future, and even though no one knows for sure when the last trumpet will sound, Paul is confident that we will be there to answer the call. In the meantime, of course, there is much work to be done. Yet because of the risen Christ, we now have the assurance that our labors are not in vain.

**Transfiguration Of The Lord
(Last Sunday After Epiphany)
2 Corinthians 3:12—4:2**

The Glory That Shines Within

Several years ago, in an attempt to provide some shade for the house, my wife and I planted two trees in the front yard. I noticed this last March, though, that one of them had suddenly died. I say "suddenly" — to be honest, I'm not sure exactly when it died. As you know, there's not much difference between a bare tree and a dead one during the winter — at least not as far as the eye can tell. You only learn the difference (as I did) with the coming of spring, when all of the other trees begin to leaf out and one is left behind in the general green onrush of new life.

The Apostle Paul uses a slightly different analogy in this passage, but I think he makes a similar point. You see, for centuries the Jewish people had lived under the requirements of the old covenant. It was designed to give them an identity, so that they could serve as an example for the other nations. However, instead of lifting them up, all it really did was to show how often they fell short. In other words, the law could describe sin, but it couldn't deter it.

Of course, no one realized this deficiency at the time — for the same reason, I suppose, that it's so difficult to tell if a tree is dead in the middle of winter. You only recognize something like that with the coming of spring. And for Paul, spring arrived in the person of Jesus Christ. It's the life he offered us in the new covenant that finally demonstrated how dead and barren the old covenant truly was. But the Israelites couldn't see that. In fact, adds Paul, "To this very day, when they hear the reading of the old covenant, that same veil is still there, since only in Christ is it set aside" (v. 14).

The veil of which Paul speaks is a reference to the story in Exodus 34, after Moses had had a conversation with the Almighty face-to-face. He didn't actually *see* God's face, mind you. Because it was believed in those days that no one could do that and live to tell about it. But Moses had been permitted to see God's back, and that was apparently close enough that some of God's glory rubbed off on him. When he came down from the mountain, he literally returned with glowing reports.

His face was shining, and as a result, the people were scared to death. This is understandable, considering what they had been doing while Moses and God were discussing the commandments. They had been busy trying to create their own god and compose their own rules. But they knew now, that, no matter how much they polished that silly golden calf, it was never going to shine as brightly as Moses' face. It was as if he had been given God's own personal spotlight, in order to bring a little of the divine presence right into their midst. No wonder the Israelites were intimidated. Some bowed their heads, others quickly buried theirs in shame, but no one was willing to *face* Moses, so to speak. He finally had to put on a veil, just to shield them from it.

The book of Exodus never really explains why he did this. Maybe he didn't want the people to be so frightened, or perhaps he was tired of them all staring and pointing at him. Whatever the actual reason may have been, Paul interprets this to mean that the afterglow of his visit with God was already beginning to fade. The way he saw it, Moses put the veil over his face "to keep the people of Israel from gazing at the end of the glory that was being set aside" (v. 12). Only they didn't realize that it was being set aside, because "their minds were hardened" (v. 14). It's almost as if they were the ones who had been wearing the veil. And as far as Paul is concerned, they never bothered to take it off. "But when one turns to the Lord," he announces, "the veil is removed" (v. 16). For in Jesus Christ, we behold God's full glory — the *Shekinah* in the flesh.

No one knows for sure whether Paul was thinking about the story of the Transfiguration when he wrote this, but he might have because it obviously fits. The mountain Jesus happened to be standing on was in Israel instead of Egypt, but it was clearly the same glory that enveloped him. As Peter, James, and John watched him pray, suddenly Jesus' entire appearance began to change. Matthew says that his face "shone like the sun" (Matthew 17:2), and his garments started to sparkle with a brilliant, dazzling whiteness, like a lightning bolt suspended in midair, crackling with power. He stood there talking with Moses and Elijah, the symbolic representatives of the law and the prophetic tradition. Luke reports that they were discussing Jesus' death, which sounds like a rather morbid topic for such a high and holy moment. But even this was not enough to dim the light within that blazing circle.

Unlike Moses, however, when Jesus came down from the mountain, his face returned to normal. It wasn't that the glory faded from his face. It was more that God took it and tucked it inside him, perhaps to find out if people would still be able to discern that shining aura without the visual aid. To put it another way, instead of wearing the light, he actually became it. He wasn't merely reflecting God's glory, like Moses had. Now it radiated out from within him. And from then on, just beneath his humanness, there burned an unmistakable holiness.

If you ask me, something of this same holiness burns inside all of us. Only it takes a special vision to see it. A few years ago, the preacher John Claypool introduced me to an old book titled *On Loving God* by Bernard of Clairvaux. Bernard was a monk who lived during the twelfth century, and he became intrigued by the thought that some of his fellow monks seemed able to recognize holiness all around them. Even the most mundane of tasks took on a sacred significance. However, for some reason, other monks were blind to this dimension of life. They walked around as if they were wearing a veil. To them it was just the same meaningless chores and rituals, day after wearisome day. Bernard began to wonder what accounted for this difference, and after much study and prayer, he came up with a fourfold continuum of successive stages toward spiritual enlightenment.

Bernard describes stage one as *the love of self for self's sake*. The psychological term for this, of course, would be narcissism. It's where each of us begins the human journey. Infants and small children, for example, tend to be notoriously self-absorbed. It's always "gimme, gimme, gimme." And to be honest, some folks never really move much past this point. They remain imprisoned in the solitary confinement of their own egos. But, thankfully, most of us realize that there is more to life than satisfying our own basic needs, so we choose to keep growing.

The second stage is what Bernard calls *the love of God for self's sake*. Notice that there is now at least the awareness of an outside reality. However, the focus is still very much on ourselves. That is, we love God to the extent that the Almighty can help us to fulfill our own agendas. As a result, all of our prayers are sprinkled with personal requests — "Lord, grant me this ... protect me from that ... allow me to have the desires of my heart." This is probably the stage that a lot of us get stuck at, but it can be terribly frustrating if we try to stay here. Ultimately, God's ways are not our own. God's timing was never meant to conform to our schedules, nor does God exist only to solve our problems and serve our plans. It's the other way around. To be sure, the love of God for self's sake represents significant progress over the childish narcissism of love of self for self's sake. But in the end, it's a relationship which is just as manipulative and utilitarian.

Bernard's third stage marks a quantum leap forward. He refers to it as *the love of God for God's sake*. It's at this point that we begin to appreciate that God has value, not in terms of what God can do for us, but simply because of who God is. When we reach this stage, prayer suddenly involves more than presenting the Almighty with a wish list, or trying to barter for a few extra blessings. It becomes a time filled with wonder and awe. After all, God didn't have to create any of us. The very fact that we exist in the first place ought to elicit endless songs of praise. To be able to accept our lives as a gift, without having to ask what other options are available, is to express this kind of love.

John Claypool tells the beautiful story of a time when his daughter was about four years old. He was hard at work in his study, when she quietly slipped in — still in her pajamas — and without a word, climbed up into his lap and laid her head on his shoulder.

"Well, this is a pleasant surprise," he said to her. "What can I do for you?"

She paused for a moment and then said, "I don't need anything right now, Daddy. I just wanted to be close to you, that's all."[1]

Claypool goes on to reflect that the preciousness of that moment was found in the fact that his daughter wasn't out on some utilitarian mission. Nor was she trying to soften him up in the hope of obtaining a future favor. Her sole agenda was the sheer joy of being with her father. And yet, how many of us ever come into God's presence with a spirit like that? Most of the time we're only interested in seeing if God would be willing to endorse our latest proposal. Even when we pray, "Thy will be done," we usually submit a few of our own recommendations along with the request. God listens patiently, of course. But I often wonder if what the Almighty is really waiting for is to have someone come with no other purpose than to say, "I just want to be close to you, Lord. That's all." To do so is to love God for God's sake.

You would think that this would be the highest level of spiritual enlightenment. However, for Bernard, it is only the third stage. There remains a fourth. Do you want to know what it is? *The love of self for God's sake.* It's when we begin to see ourselves as God sees us. It's the ability, not just to accept ourselves, but to celebrate our existence. A lot of us have never done that before, or if we have it's with great difficulty and reluctance. Sometimes we won't even allow another person to celebrate our existence. They'll pay us a wonderful compliment for something we've done, and we immediately begin to hem and haw. "Oh, it was nothing," we'll say. "Don't mention it." But why not mention it? In fact, why not affirm it? Why are we constantly discounting our own value? The book of Genesis says that when humankind was created, we were fashioned in God's own image. In effect, we are God's signature piece. Isn't that worth celebrating?

The Apostle Paul puts it like this, "All of us, with unveiled faces, seeing the glory of the Lord as though reflected in a mirror, are being transformed into the same image from one degree of glory to another" (v. 18). In other words, no matter how tarnished the image becomes, there burns within each of us an unmistakable holiness. And every once in a while, we catch a glimpse of this glory. We look across the dinner table at a face we've seen 1,000 times before, only this time we behold something so vibrant, so incandescent, so shimmering with life, that we can't help but feel we've witnessed a transfiguration of sorts. Of course, the person's face may return to normal the very next moment, the same way Jesus' did. But that doesn't mean the glory faded. It's always shining just beneath the surface.

Jesus told us, "You are the light of the world" (Matthew 5:14) — and it's worth noting the verb he uses there. He didn't say, "You *could be* the light," or "If you work at it hard enough, you *might be* the light." He said we already *are* the light of the world. Only if you can't see that in yourself, then chances are you'll probably be blind to it most everywhere else, too.

Bernard was absolutely correct. The love of self for God's sake is the highest level of spiritual enlightenment. It's when we finally recognize ourselves as glorious beings — as a "treasure in clay jars," says Paul (2 Corinthians 4:7) — that we begin to see the holiness all around us. It's almost as if a veil is removed, and the whole world suddenly starts shining with the new life of spring.

---

1. John Claypool, *Stories Jesus Still Tells: The Parables* (New York: McCracken Press, 1993), p. 16.

Lectionary Preaching After Pentecost

The following index will aid the user of this book in matching the correct Sunday with the appropriate text during Pentecost. All texts in this book are from the series for the Second Readings, Revised Common Lectionary. (Note that the ELCA division of Lutheranism is now following the Revised Common Lectionary.) The Lutheran designations indicate days comparable to Sundays on which Revised Common Lectionary Propers or Ordinary Time designations are used.

(Fixed dates do not pertain to Lutheran Lectionary)

Fixed Date Lectionaries
*Revised Common (including ELCA)
and Roman Catholic*

Lutheran Lectionary
Lutheran

Fixed Date Lectionaries	Lutheran Lectionary
The Day of Pentecost	The Day of Pentecost
The Holy Trinity	The Holy Trinity
May 29-June 4 — Proper 4, Ordinary Time 9	Pentecost 2
June 5-11 — Proper 5, Ordinary Time 10	Pentecost 3
June 12-18 — Proper 6, Ordinary Time 11	Pentecost 4
June 19-25 — Proper 7, Ordinary Time 12	Pentecost 5
June 26-July 2 — Proper 8, Ordinary Time 13	Pentecost 6
July 3-9 — Proper 9, Ordinary Time 14	Pentecost 7
July 10-16 — Proper 10, Ordinary Time 15	Pentecost 8
July 17-23 — Proper 11, Ordinary Time 16	Pentecost 9
July 24-30 — Proper 12, Ordinary Time 17	Pentecost 10
July 31-Aug. 6 — Proper 13, Ordinary Time 18	Pentecost 11
Aug. 7-13 — Proper 14, Ordinary Time 19	Pentecost 12
Aug. 14-20 — Proper 15, Ordinary Time 20	Pentecost 13
Aug. 21-27 — Proper 16, Ordinary Time 21	Pentecost 14
Aug. 28-Sept. 3 — Proper 17, Ordinary Time 22	Pentecost 15
Sept. 4-10 — Proper 18, Ordinary Time 23	Pentecost 16
Sept. 11-17 — Proper 19, Ordinary Time 24	Pentecost 17
Sept. 18-24 — Proper 20, Ordinary Time 25	Pentecost 18

Sept. 25-Oct. 1 — Proper 21, Ordinary Time 26	Pentecost 19
Oct. 2-8 — Proper 22, Ordinary Time 27	Pentecost 20
Oct. 9-15 — Proper 23, Ordinary Time 28	Pentecost 21
Oct. 16-22 — Proper 24, Ordinary Time 29	Pentecost 22
Oct. 23-29 — Proper 25, Ordinary Time 30	Pentecost 23
Oct. 30-Nov. 5 — Proper 26, Ordinary Time 31	Pentecost 24
Nov. 6-12 — Proper 27, Ordinary Time 32	Pentecost 25
Nov. 13-19 — Proper 28, Ordinary Time 33	Pentecost 26
	Pentecost 27
Nov. 20-26 — Christ The King	Christ The King

Reformation Day (or last Sunday in October) is October 31 (Revised Common, Lutheran)

All Saints' Day (or first Sunday in November) is November 1 (Revised Common, Lutheran, Roman Catholic)

U.S. / Canadian Lectionary Comparison

The following index shows the correlation between the Sundays and special days of the church year as they are titled or labeled in the Revised Common Lectionary published by the Consultation On Common Texts and used in the United States (the reference used for this book) and the Sundays and special days of the church year as they are titled or labeled in the Revised Common Lectionary used in Canada.

Revised Common Lectionary	**Canadian Revised Common Lectionary**
Advent 1	Advent 1
Advent 2	Advent 2
Advent 3	Advent 3
Advent 4	Advent 4
Christmas Eve	Christmas Eve
Nativity Of The Lord / Christmas Day	The Nativity Of Our Lord
Christmas 1	Christmas 1
January 1 / Holy Name of Jesus	January 1 / The Name Of Jesus
Christmas 2	Christmas 2
Epiphany Of The Lord	The Epiphany Of Our Lord
Baptism Of The Lord / Epiphany 1	The Baptism Of Our Lord / Proper 1
Epiphany 2 / Ordinary Time 2	Epiphany 2 / Proper 2
Epiphany 3 / Ordinary Time 3	Epiphany 3 / Proper 3
Epiphany 4 / Ordinary Time 4	Epiphany 4 / Proper 4
Epiphany 5 / Ordinary Time 5	Epiphany 5 / Proper 5
Epiphany 6 / Ordinary Time 6	Epiphany 6 / Proper 6
Epiphany 7 / Ordinary Time 7	Epiphany 7 / Proper 7
Epiphany 8 / Ordinary Time 8	Epiphany 8 / Proper 8
Transfiguration Of The Lord / Last Sunday After Epiphany	The Transfiguration Of Our Lord / Last Sunday After Epiphany
Ash Wednesday	Ash Wednesday
Lent 1	Lent 1
Lent 2	Lent 2
Lent 3	Lent 3
Lent 4	Lent 4
Lent 5	Lent 5
Passion / Palm Sunday (Lent 6)	Passion / Palm Sunday
Holy / Maundy Thursday	Holy / Maundy Thursday
Good Friday	Good Friday
Resurrection Of The Lord / Easter	The Resurrection Of Our Lord

Easter 2	Easter 2
Easter 3	Easter 3
Easter 4	Easter 4
Easter 5	Easter 5
Easter 6	Easter 6
Ascension Of The Lord	The Ascension Of Our Lord
Easter 7	Easter 7
Day Of Pentecost	The Day Of Pentecost
Trinity Sunday	The Holy Trinity
Proper 4 / Pentecost 2 / O T 9*	Proper 9
Proper 5 / Pent 3 / O T 10	Proper 10
Proper 6 / Pent 4 / O T 11	Proper 11
Proper 7 / Pent 5 / O T 12	Proper 12
Proper 8 / Pent 6 / O T 13	Proper 13
Proper 9 / Pent 7 / O T 14	Proper 14
Proper 10 / Pent 8 / O T 15	Proper 15
Proper 11 / Pent 9 / O T 16	Proper 16
Proper 12 / Pent 10 / O T 17	Proper 17
Proper 13 / Pent 11 / O T 18	Proper 18
Proper 14 / Pent 12 / O T 19	Proper 19
Proper 15 / Pent 13 / O T 20	Proper 20
Proper 16 / Pent 14 / O T 21	Proper 21
Proper 17 / Pent 15 / O T 22	Proper 22
Proper 18 / Pent 16 / O T 23	Proper 23
Proper 19 / Pent 17 / O T 24	Proper 24
Proper 20 / Pent 18 / O T 25	Proper 25
Proper 21 / Pent 19 / O T 26	Proper 26
Proper 22 / Pent 20 / O T 27	Proper 27
Proper 23 / Pent 21 / O T 28	Proper 28
Proper 24 / Pent 22 / O T 29	Proper 29
Proper 25 / Pent 23 / O T 30	Proper 30
Proper 26 / Pent 24 / O T 31	Proper 31
Proper 27 / Pent 25 / O T 32	Proper 32
Proper 28 / Pent 26 / O T 33	Proper 33
Christ The King (Proper 29 / O T 34)	Proper 34 / Christ The King / Reign Of Christ
Reformation Day (October 31)	Reformation Day (October 31)
All Saints' Day (November 1 or 1st Sunday in November)	All Saints' Day (November 1)
Thanksgiving Day (4th Thursday of November)	Thanksgiving Day (2nd Monday of October)

*O T = Ordinary Time